Wine
STYLE

Discover the wines
you will love through
50 simple recipes

Wine
STYLE

Kate Leahy

Photographs by Erin Scott

TEN SPEED PRESS
California | New York

CONTENTS

Introduction 1

Wine Basics

WINE TEXTURES AND FLAVORS 6

HOW WINE IS MADE 12

BUYING WINE 16

WINE AND FOOD 22

COOKING FROM THIS BOOK 25

Recipes

SPARKLING WINES 34

CRISP WHITE WINES 50

RICH WHITE WINES 64

ORANGE WINES 82

ROSÉ WINES 94

PICNIC RED WINES 106

REASONABLY SERIOUS RED WINES 122

BIG RED WINES 136

SWEET WINES 150

About the Author 166

Acknowledgments 167

Index 168

INTRODUCTION

In a Tesco grocery store in Exeter, England, there it was: a bottle of white wine labeled "Great with Chicken." No grape, no location, just "Great with Chicken." The shop was down the hill from the university I attended that year, and I was the target market—an indiscriminate undergrad on a budget. Still, that bottle left me with more questions than answers: Why chicken? Any kind of chicken? Was there a magical flavor in the bottle that made it so great *with* chicken?

There is, of course, plenty of wine that qualifies as the opposite of "Great with Chicken." It might come with an information-overload wine label, the bottle described in such a way to ensure you can't do it justice unless you roast a whole duck over cherry-wood lump charcoal and serve it strewed with fermented nettles and sea buckthorn berries. But drinking wine you like, with food you like, doesn't have to be either extreme. This book is about finding the happy middle ground, the wines that charm you with food to eat alongside and make the exploration more fun.

My own understanding of wine started when I was about eight years old, on a family road trip to the Napa Valley. Back then, Napa didn't have nearly as many wineries as it does today, and for my parents, this trip was as much about having a picnic as it was about tasting wine. We tumbled out of the back of a sticky Chevy station wagon into a parking lot off Highway 29, already cranky from what was only an hour's drive. My brother, sister, and I filed into a cool tasting room that smelled of wet stone, and while my parents sampled the local red, the staff offered me a glass of slightly frothy homemade grape juice.

I took a big sip and spit it back into my cup. Made from what I now believe were wine grapes left over from harvest, it was sharp, sour, and had most likely started to ferment. According to my eight-year-old self, this was not grape juice! It would take me years to realize that juice that is a little fizzy and unexpected is actually way better than the plain ol' purple stuff. We all start somewhere.

Back then, wine drinking for grown-ups was simple. My parents, who cut their teeth on sweet bottles of Blue Nun in college, had graduated to buying wine from the local grocery store, where an enterprising staffer would announce a deal on a case over the loudspeaker. This kicked off a stampede of shopping carts to the far side of the store as customers loaded up on whatever he was offering. The loudspeaker specials always sold out, and everyone trusted the wine guy to make the decisions easy for them. Most of the time, the decision was easy—a bottle of white or a bottle of red, something charming for everyday occasions. What's changed since those days is selection and information. Wines can be white or red, sure, but they can also be pink, orange, sparkling, sweet—or nearly all of those at once. There's a style to suit any taste, though the irony is that the bottles I love to drink today may not be so different from the lighter, everyday wines my parents bought by the caseload from their favorite grocery-store wine guy.

Years after that grumpy family trip to Napa, I ended up living there, cooking professionally and turning into a casual observer of the rhythms of summer tourism and fall grape harvests. My fellow line cooks and I couldn't really afford to drink the local wine— most of it Cabernet Sauvignon—so we stuck with bottles of picnic-style reds that friends made on the side for themselves. When I was at work on a hot summer day, one of those bottles exploded in my tiny studio apartment—my first lesson on the effects of what happens when a wine is bottled before it has finished fermenting and then starts to ferment again when the room temperature reaches above 90°F. (Today, making wine that finishes its fermentation in the bottle is done intentionally, but the bottles are stoppered in a way that prevents such explosions.)

It was only after moving to San Francisco and taking a job at A16, a restaurant known for its extensive collection of southern Italian wines, that I had an opportunity to taste a wide range of styles. The best part was that I could do this without any expectation of expertise—at the time, no one else knew much about the wines made in Campania, the region encompassing Naples, so rather than feel pressured to judge one bottle as superior to another, I started to think of how wines fell into certain styles. Nearly all styles—from bone-dry sparklers to deep reds and the rare dessert wine—had a place. Though as a line cook, the wines I gravitated toward most back then were lean, savory, and slightly chilled—kitchen work is hot and messy, and sometimes you just need refreshment.

Today, most of the wines I seek out fall into the "charming and affordable" camp, the kind of wines that make people smile without taking over the conversation. Friends I've known from childhood get together once a month for what we call Porch Time. The idea started as a joke (none of us had porches), but the name lost its irony ages ago, and some of us have graduated to homes with backyards, if not quite porches. Porch Time usually hinges around a potluck mishmash of things we are able to scavenge together paired with a bottle of affordable wine. Most of the food at these events can be served at room temperature, with maybe one or two things coming hot from

the oven. And since Porch Time was born around tiny apartment kitchens, the recipes we relied on needed to be made without a lot of extra fuss. Popcorn, some good cheeses and salumi, olives, and store-bought hummus all helped fuel our conversations.

This book is for occasions like that: porch times, game nights, picnics, book clubs, hangout sessions, or any other excuse to get together with friends. Some recipes take longer than others, but most hinge on curating food with the wine to facilitate sharing and exploring. There are no "Great with Chicken" rules here (pretty much any wine can be "great" with chicken, depending on how you season the bird). Instead, it's about reclaiming the idea that any time we can get together with friends and family is worth celebrating—now more than ever. Taste, explore, form opinions, and have fun while you're doing so.

USING THIS BOOK

The recipes in this book are organized by wine style, from sparkling and crisp white wines to the deepest, richest reds and dessert wines, with a few outliers (orange wines, although they are made with white grapes, can be more intense than red wines). If you have a bottle in hand and want to know what to serve with it, you can turn to the section of the book about that wine style. And if you like a certain recipe but haven't picked out a wine, you can read the recipe for suggestions on wines that make for delightful matches. Many of the recipes work for a range of wine styles, so don't let the chapters constrain you.

Wine Basics

Wine Textures and Flavors

Maybe you've just picked out a bottle of Pinot Noir from Oregon because you've tried it in the past and liked it. Great! But what is it about *that* bottle of Pinot Noir that you particularly like?

Learning to identify the flavors and textures of that wine will help you discover other bottles you'll like that share a similar style. Grapes are the chameleons of the fruit world. Once their juices are fermented into wine, they evoke aromas and flavors that resemble everything from white peach and orange blossoms to black pepper and black olives. Grapes also yield wines in a range of textures and sensations, from bright and bubbly to rich and silky. That's why tasting notes and wine descriptions on the back of a bottle, in a shop, or online can be valuable for helping to anticipate what to expect from an unfamiliar wine.

Some tasting notes are easy to understand, while others need a little deciphering. For instance, when wine pros say a wine tastes like black cherries, they're implying that there is something in each sip that reminds them of sweet-tart, inky cherries—not that the wine tastes exactly like eating handfuls of the fresh fruit—or that it was made from any fruit other than grapes. Once you've noticed the same cherry-like flavor in a few glasses of red wine, this description gets easier to understand, and you can start to anticipate what a wine will taste like based on the tasting notes. But when notes describe a wine as resembling pebbles bathed by moonlight or liken a bottle to a chunky-knit sweater, it's easy to lose the plot.

To break things down, it helps to get a little familiar with what tannins, minerality, fruitiness, and earthiness actually mean. ("Pebbles in moonlight?" Maybe the wine has a stony, mineral-like flavor that would make it perfect with briny oysters. "Chunky sweater?" The wine could be rich and warming—and high in alcohol, the kind to pour on a cozy, cold night.) A wine often encompasses more than one texture and flavor category. A fruity red wine can also be big, and a white wine with a lot of acidity can also have a mineral or salty accent. No matter whether they are lean or big, acidic or tannic, the best wines find harmony among all of these categories.

TEXTURE CATEGORIES
(what the wine feels like in your mouth)

Acidity

Some wines have a refreshing brightness to them. They quench your thirst at the end of a long day and keep your taste buds alive during a meal. On the pH scale, these wines are more acidic than other wines, and at their best they can help balance out food just like a squeeze of lemon juice can perk up a bowl of soup. Acidity is often attributed to sparkling and lighter white wines, but red and rosé wines can also carry a lot of acidity. Natural wines also often have more acidity than their classic counterparts.

Acidic wines tend to be lower in alcohol than bigger wines and feel thinner on your tongue. They also make your mouth water, but not in a way that leaves it feeling dry, unlike tannins (see right). They are the only way to go when serving foods that are also high in acidity, like salad or citrus, because they balance each other. Wines with bright, refreshing acidity are often my favorites, especially because they are the easiest ones to drink with food.

————————————

Wines with acidity can be described as

bracing - brisk - cool-climate - crisp - crunchy - edgy - fresh - high-acid - mouthpuckering - nervous - racy - searing - volatile (once considered a flaw, some volatile acidity has become more accepted) - zippy

————————————

Tannins

Have you ever brewed black tea and then forgotten to take the tea leaves out? The way that drinking overbrewed tea can dry out the surface of your tongue is the effect of tannins. They make your mouth water and your tongue tighten. Tannins can come from grape skins, seeds, stems, and even barrels, adding texture and structure to red and orange wines. White and rosé wines are made in ways that minimize contact with grape skins and seeds, most of them don't factor into the tannin conversation. Some grapes are notorious for being high in tannins (a grape in northeast Italy is called Tazzelenghe, which means "tongue cutter" precisely for that reason), while others, like Pinot Noir, have delicate tannins. Tannic wines often taste harsh when young but also can age much longer, as the tannins themselves turn velvety or, at the very least, are gentler on the tongue, almost like adding milk to that overbrewed tea. While tannins can feel like they're scrubbing your mouth, tannic wines make great partners with steak and other rich food, keeping your palate alive much like wines that are high in acidity.

————————————

Wines with tannins can be described as

angular - astringent - bitter - chewy - drying - extracted - fine (when tannins are more integrated and less noticeable) - grippy - harsh (when tannins feel out of balance or are very pronounced) - structured - velvety (often used to describe older wines)

————————————

Body

When you pour a glass of natural almond milk next to a glass of heavy cream, the almond milk looks thin, while the cream coats the glass. They also feel differently on your tongue; the almond milk lightly coats your mouth, if at all, while the cream lingers much longer. The difference in viscosity between the two glasses is similar to the difference you see among various wines. Wines that physically feel lighter in your mouth have more acidity and less alcohol than richer, bigger wines, and the lightest of all are sparkling. Color can also offer a clue. A pale pink rosé is translucent, while a deep purple Zinfandel coats the inside of the glass. A Pinot Noir that is lighter in a glass than a Syrah will also taste lighter, so Syrah would be the "bigger" wine in this comparison. A lot of factors contribute to body, from the region where the grapes are grown (warm, sunny climates often yield bigger wines) to how the wine was aged (newer oak barrels can impart richness). Even if a wine doesn't have residual sugar (see Sweetness, page 165), bigger wines often taste sweeter. Match big wines with bold foods so neither is overshadowed. Wines that feel denser in your mouth can also be higher in alcohol. If the alcohol feels disjointed compared with the flavors, a wine is often called "hot."

Lighter-bodied wines can be described as

cool - effervescent - fresh - lean - taut - unoaked

Richer-bodied wines can be described as

big - hot (if the alcohol is out of balance or very high) - luscious - oaky/oaked - oily - ripe - sunny

Other terms that help decipher body

Malo (short for "malolactic fermentation"): when sharper, brighter malic acid in wine is converted to mellower lactic acid for a rounder, richer wine. Sur lie/on the lees: wine that has aged with dead yeast cells left from fermentation—this can add body to wine, even lean wines such as Muscadet.

FLAVOR CATEGORIES
(what the wine smells and tastes like)

Fruity

When it comes to easy-to-drink wines, fruit flavors and aromas are often the first thing you notice. Some wines taste tropical, some conjure up apples and pears, and others are reminiscent of berry jam. I've encountered tasting notes that read like a recipe for fruit salad, while others simply state "citrus," "red fruit," or "black fruit" ("red fruit" means raspberries, strawberries, red cherries, and red currants, while "black fruit" means blackberries, black currants, and black cherries). The flavor of the wine isn't always in line with what a wine looks like. "Banana" is sometimes used to describe red wines made by carbonic maceration (a method of fermenting grapes in whole grape bunches in a sealed tank without oxygen that is most associated with Beaujolais Nouveau). So don't be surprised if a glass of a light red wine greets you with a whiff of banana now and again.

——————————————

Fruity white wine notes

apple - apricot - citrus peel/zest - grapefruit - lemon/lemon drop - lychee - melon - quince - pear - pineapple - white peach

Fruity lighter-style red wine notes

banana - blueberry - cranberry - raspberry - red cherry - red currant - rhubarb - strawberry

Fruity denser/darker-style red wine notes

blackberry - black cherry - black currant - plum - prune/dried fruit - stewed/cooked fruit

——————————————

Earthy

When a wine smells and tastes less like fruit and more like forest, it's probably an earthy wine. It could be an older bottle that's lost some of its fruitiness, but it's most likely from a part of the world known for earthy wine. If you like this style, look toward cooler climates in Europe, particularly France, and anywhere that has a long history of eating mushrooms and truffles—in those areas, the wines have evolved to complement these earthy ingredients. Red Burgundy is one of the most famous earthy, complex wines, though not all earthy wines are as rare and expensive.

——————————————

Earthy wine notes

beet - cedar shavings - forest floor - leather - mushroom - potting clay - tar/wet asphalt - tobacco - walnut

——————————————

Minerality

Spend any time with winemakers and sommeliers and you'll feel as though you should have earned a degree in geology. It doesn't take too long before limestone, sandstone, or volcanic rock comes up in conversation. With all other variables being equal (same winemaking methods, same grape, same farming, same climate), grapes grown in different soils on top of different types of bedrock can make profoundly different wines. Sometimes, these wines carry a salty, briny, or stony taste. Wines made in Portugal, Greece, Liguria, Sicily, or other areas along the Mediterranean coast can actually taste salty because of the salt carried in sea breezes. Mineral-tinged wines are happy matches with food because they provide subtle seasoning. If you like these wines, look for bottle descriptions that mention "briny" or "minerality" in the tasting notes.

———————————

Mineral wine notes

chalk - flint - oyster shell/seashell - salt/saline - slate/wet slate - wet stone/wet rock

———————————

Herbal/Floral

A close cousin to earthy and mineral, this category of wine descriptions is also closely linked to nature. Some grape varieties, like Gewürztraminer, are naturally aromatic. And some vineyards yield grapes with herbal or floral accents thanks to their unique microclimate and soil. (In tasting notes, it's actually common for winemakers to reference the wildflowers and other plants that grow near their vines.) Wines with herbal accents can taste layered and complex, with subtle floral aromas. But some floral wines can hit you over the head with an exuberantly aromatic bouquet. The aroma of these wines doesn't always match the taste, but at their best, herbal and/or floral wines carry a combination of aromas and flavors that keep you coming back for more.

———————————

Herbal wine notes

anise/fennel/licorice - bay laurel - black pepper/white pepper - chamomile - eucalyptus - grass - green bell pepper/red bell pepper/capsicum - green olive/black olive - juniper - sage/oregano/thyme/mint - tomato leaf

Floral wine notes

geranium - honeysuckle - jasmine - orange blossom - rose/dried rose petal - violet

———————————

How Wine Is Made

Experts will tell you that good wine comes from good grapes grown in the right places that are then gently transformed into wine. Still, when buying wine, it's helpful to know some of the basics of what happens after those grapes are harvested.

No matter the skin color, most winemaking grapes have clear juice. The biggest difference among red, orange, rosé, and white wines results from the contact between grape skins and juices. A red wine is produced from red grapes, but if the skins are whisked away right after the grapes are pressed, the wine will be white. (That's how you get blanc de noirs in Champagne, a clear sparkling wine made from red grapes.) If the skins stay with the juices after the grapes are pressed and while the wine ferments, the juices absorb color and tannins. Some grape skins have more tannins, and other grape skins have more pigment. Grape stems also have tannins, and winemakers can choose to leave the stems in place or remove them or keep the grapes in whole bunches as they ferment—all of this comes down to a winemaker's choice. Even seeds impart tannins to the wine, and they are removed together with the skins. With white wines, the juices are often fermented after they've been separated from the skins to preserve fresh, juicy flavor without any bitterness from the skins. (See more about orange wines on page 83 and rosé wines on page 95.)

Grape juices start to ferment thanks to ambient yeasts in the air or cultured yeasts added to the fermenting tank. The yeasts eat the grape sugars, turning them into alcohol. After several days or a few weeks, depending on the wine, the yeasts finish their sugar feast and the wine is either drained off the skins (for red wines) or the clear wine at the top is transferred to another vessel (for typical white wines). For some white wines, this step happens a little later so the wine can linger a bit longer on the spent yeast cells, called lees. This gives the wine a richer flavor and can help preserve the wine so it can age longer (labels may say sur lie, "on the lees," if this is the case).

Eventually, the wines are bottled, though there may be several steps in between. Some wines go through malolactic fermentation ("malo"), a process in which sharp malic acid (as in a green apple) is converted to softer lactic acid. This is common in red wines and has become typical in richer white wines, like California Chardonnay. It often happens naturally either during or after fermentation from a bacteria that lives in many wineries, though some winemakers actively avoid it to keep a wine's acidity levels high. Wines may also be blended at this point, with the fermented juices of one grape variety or specific vineyard mixed with another to achieve balance.

Some wine descriptions mention the vessels used to age the wine. Stainless steel is neutral, allowing the wine to age but not imparting flavor, and it often indicates wines that are more about freshness and fruit. Old oak barrels (sometimes referred to as "neutral oak") give wine minimal flavor but allow it to breathe as it ages. New oak barrels impart the most flavor—many think too much. Some wines are aged both in barrels and in bottles before being released, like Barolo and Champagne, while others go from tank to bottle to market in a matter of months, like Prosecco. It all depends on the style.

EUROPE VERSUS EVERYONE ELSE
(Old World and New World)

"Grape or Place" is the name of a silly game I invented and then forced upon my mom. I said a wine word and she had to tell me if it was the name of a grape or a place. It went something like this: "Barolo," I said. "Grape!" she answered. "Barbaresco," I said. "Grape!" she said again. "Nebbiolo," I continued. "Place!" Her answers were incorrect, confirming that the game was no fun for the same reasons that wine snobbery is no fun.

Still, "Grape or Place" illustrates the difference between wines made in European countries where wine grapes have grown since Greek or Roman times—the so-called Old World—and wines made outside of Europe—aka the New World. Old World/European wines are often (though certainly not always) named for the place from which they come, while New World wines tend to be named after the grape. With my game, Barolo and Barbaresco are historic areas in Italy's Piedmont region. The grape that goes into these wines is Nebbiolo, one of Italy's most important wine grapes. Only Nebbiolo grapes grown in the Barolo area can make a Barolo wine. Nebbiolo wine can be made elsewhere but can't go by the name Barolo. Along the same line, France makes red Burgundy, a wine named after a place, and Oregon grows Pinot Noir, the very same grape used in red Burgundy. But Oregon Pinot Noir can never be called Burgundy, the place. Wines named after grape varieties don't always indicate that a wine is from outside of Europe, but it is one of the differentiating factors.

But back to the idea of an old and a new world of wine: Although it is still common practice to call wines made in Europe "Old World" and wines made everywhere else "New World," it's time to move beyond these generalizations. For starters, the origins of wine fall outside of Europe's borders. Archaeologists have found evidence of winemaking in Armenia, the country of Georgia, and Iran dating back roughly 6,000 years, and Israel has records of winemaking going back 5,000 years, well before vines were grown throughout continental Europe. In more recent history, consider that Chile and South Africa both have had vineyards since the sixteenth century. Should these countries be called "New World" regions all these centuries later?

Still, because this is such a common way to see wine described, it's worth knowing the difference between the two styles. When someone says a wine tastes like it's made in an Old World style (no matter where it's from), this means it exhibits a grounded, earthy, or mineral character. The wine may have flavors of fruit, like red cherries or strawberries, but fruit is not the first thing you notice. The wine itself may be made in a more traditional way, evoking images of enormous Slavonian oak barrels resting in the bowels of an ancient monastery. By comparison, New World wines are characterized as being fruity and round, sometimes as smooth as an electric car. Over time, the style division between the old and new worlds has blurred, and there are now winemakers in Oregon, California, Australia, and elsewhere striving to produce wine in a more grounded, "Old World" style, while some winemakers in Italy, France, and Spain are going for a more fruit-forward style.

The key distinction to remember is when a wine is described as Old World, the fruit flavors will be more restrained, while a wine characterized as New World in style will be more extroverted, with fruit right up front.

NATURAL WINE

For the past couple of decades, one of the biggest debates in the wine world has focused on the philosophy of low-intervention winemaking. Natural wine is to classic or conventional wine what sourdough bread is to bread made with commercial yeast. By using commercial yeast, it's easier to control the variables and achieve consistent results every time you make a recipe. With sourdough, bread takes time and each loaf varies. Yet despite the challenges, sourdough has a passionate fan base of bakers and eaters. And natural wine has an equally obsessive group of makers and drinkers. They champion countries such as Georgia that never stopped making wine in ancient ways (the country is known for orange wines made in clay qvevri, a vessel similar to an amphora).

Instead of commercial yeasts, natural winemakers let native yeasts naturally found in the winery or on the grapes themselves start fermentation. No enzymes or other things are added to help the wine along, and it's never filtered or fined, processes that remove tiny particles. Many natural winemakers also avoid adding sulfur or only add a small amount right before bottling to help preserve the wine. (Since sulfur occurs naturally in wine, even wines made without additional sulfur will still have "contains sulfites" on the label.) Winemakers also avoid grapes grown with pesticides, fungicides, and herbicides and often look deeper into reviving the vitality of vineyard soils.

The key point to remember is that natural wine is not a style, it's an ideal. While some winemakers have always made wine in this low-intervention "natural" way, the movement picked up steam in the past few decades. Part of it came from scientific advancement:

by the late twentieth century, nearly any viticulture or enology issue could be corrected with chemicals, technology, or industrial farming practices. Commercial yeasts had become so specialized that the yeasts alone could determine specific aromatic or fruit flavors in wine. Plus, a host of additives were also permitted and did not need to be mentioned on a label. Winemakers started to speak out against these conventional farming and winemaking practices, taking a stand against what they argued had become a sterile mainstream beverage.

There was also an economic case to be made in favor of natural wine. In France, prized vineyard land in Burgundy and Bordeaux was unaffordable to aspiring winemakers, so they sought out overlooked places, finding corners in the Loire and the Languedoc that weren't so well-known. Natural wine can be produced on a small scale without a lot of fancy cellar equipment, so winemakers could afford to take a few risks without losing everything.

Then natural wine became cool in wine bars in cosmopolitan cities around the world. As demand grew, so did the number of natural wines entering the market, and some started tasting like they were being made to fit a specific style, funky or volatile for the sake of being different. Natural winemakers who had been crafting wine this way for years were concerned that a lot of the new natural wine was being produced for a specific style, losing a sense of place or distinct identity. Natural wine should still taste like wine, they insisted, not kombucha, not cider, not vinegar or anything else. Some sommeliers and winemakers also threw up their hands at trendy bottles and questioned if the natural wine movement would ruin a generation of palates. Let's just say the whole debate got heated.

Fortunately, the divide between natural wine and what's often called "classic" or "conventional" wine has softened. There's more room in the middle for winemakers who don't align themselves outright with the natural wine community but still strive to make wine on a human scale, crafting small batches in pragmatic ways, investing in organic or biodynamic farming practices, and minimizing the use of sulfur or other aids. The natural wine movement also helped popularize easy-drinking, low-alcohol wines, like pét nat, and introduced a new generation to orange wine, which now has more fans than ever. Thanks to natural wine, more people importing wines from Croatia, Slovenia, and Georgia find ready markets in the United States. Wine is a more diverse and interesting world today in part because of the movement. But even so, the quantity of natural wine made each year is much smaller than the percentage of attention it has garnered. Natural wines will always be made in small amounts, and that means they'll never be available everywhere, which is part of the charm.

As for color, taste, and other characteristics, natural wines vary just as much as classic or conventional wines. They can be pale yellow to inky purple and anywhere in between. Overall, though, they tend to be lower in alcohol, lighter in body, and higher in acidity. They may look cloudy or have an "off" aroma right after the bottle is opened, though that doesn't necessarily mean they're bad. If you do notice a funky smell, pour some wine into your glass, swirl it a bit, and wait a few minutes. Often the funk goes away. Sometimes a bacteria will cause the wine to taste off in a way that doesn't go away—like barnyard or Band-Aids—something that conventional winemakers usually filter out but that some natural wine enthusiasts like in small quantities. If a wine doesn't taste good to you, pass on it, but try a different bottle. It's normal to not love every wine you try, be it natural or classic.

FILTERING AND FINING

A big part of natural wine's appeal is the nothing-added/nothing-taken-away promise. For vegans and vegetarians, they can rest assured that no animal products were used to clarify the wine. Some wines go through a process of filtering or fining, which helps stabilize wine and make it clear. A fining agent is something added to wine that bonds with tiny particles and then falls to the bottom of the tank. The result is clear wine, and the fining agents themselves don't end up in the finished product. Some traditional fining agents still used today include egg whites, fish bladders, and other animal products, yet there are many other vegan-friendly alternatives, such as bentonite, a type of clay. Even among classic winemakers, fining or filtering wine can be controversial since some believe it strips the wine of character and flavor. Given time, gravity does the job without any intervention, allowing particles to naturally fall to the base of the tank, leaving a clear wine in their wake.

Buying Wine

In a perfect world, we'd all have what my parents had when I was a kid: a local wine person everyone trusted to make the decisions easy. In their case, it was a wine guy for a grocery store who used a loudspeaker to announce deals. Today, we have a lot of other ways to find our loudspeaker person, including wine shops with newsletters, searchable online wine databases, and wine clubs.

INDEPENDENT WINE SHOPS

It used to be that sommeliers in restaurants got all the credit for championing new wines, but the best independent wine shops have been doing this quietly for years, selecting wines they like and displaying descriptions next to bottles to highlight their choices. They are like the indie bookstores of the wine world, and you go to them to find bottles you wouldn't come across if browsing online. Some have collections that are all about what's new and obscure, while others go for the big-name bottles, but the best have a mix. Just like you can ask a bookstore owner for recommendations on a good summer read, a wine shop has you covered if you say you want "a light white wine with great personality" or "a juicy red wine for a picnic." They're usually happy to suggest a couple of options. Even if you live far from certain shops, you can learn a lot by signing up for their newsletters. Plus, many stores now ship farther afield. If you buy a bottle and find you like the shop's taste, consider purchasing a mixed case of six or twelve bottles—shops often offer case discounts.

INDEPENDENT GROCERY STORES

Some independent grocery stores or regional chains (the kind stocked with artisan cheeses, local breads, and single-origin chocolate bars) often have dedicated wine buyers. You can tell how many resources a store dedicates to wine if you see someone fussing over the shelves, taking the time to point out specific bottles to customers, or offering handwritten notes like the ones that independent wine shops display. Buyers for grocery stores have to work extra hard to promote unfamiliar wines—after all, their customers may have popped in to pick up eggs and toilet paper and might not want to impulse-buy col fondo Prosecco, no matter how cool it is. But they are always willing to guide you to their lesser-known treasures and can often do special orders for you.

CHAIN GROCERY STORES, DISCOUNT STORES, AND BIG-BOX RETAILERS

These are a mixed bag when it comes to wine shopping, but they are good for treasure hunting. The trick is to look out for wines you don't see there all the time. If a wine is always in stock in a big-box store, chances are that oceans of it are being made in an industrial way so it is available year-round. But if you pass the same aisles often enough, you'll notice when there's something less typical—a Muscadet in a sea of Sauvignon Blanc, say. That's when it's time to take note. A winery may have needed to clear some inventory and sold the wine to the store at a discount. Or a winery wanted to offload wine in a discreet way. If a famous red-wine producer wants to sell off its rosé for whatever reason, it can do so quickly through one of these stores, rather than watch wine retailers discount the wine in a way that hurts brand value. The lesson? When you are stocking up on a lifetime supply of paper towels or pretzels, keep an eye out for buried treasures. And skip the bottle with the beach-ball or seashell motif that you see everywhere—for a few additional dollars, you can drink something way more interesting.

WINE CLUBS

More and more wine shops and restaurants are offering clubs as a way to engage with customers, inspire them to explore new wines, and maintain steady business. Joining a club that's part of a shop or restaurant you love is an excellent way to always have a bottle of something fun to try and be part of a community. The best clubs provide tasting notes and background information that can help you learn about what's behind the bottles. There are often other benefits to memberships, such as discounts on bottles or tastings. While wine clubs from wineries can also be fun, they do limit the styles of wine you'll be able to try, so only join if you truly love the winery. Beware of clubs that promise to mail you twelve bottles of wine for steeply discounted prices from vaguely named "high-end" producers, and always read the fine print to avoid getting locked into a subscription service you can't get out of.

OTHER TIPS

Buy wines that have clear places of origin. The more specific, the better (many of the most valuable wines in the world get granular with their origins). Avoid wines that are solely labeled "Great with Chicken" for the obvious reasons.

If you discover you like a specific wine from Italy, France, or farther afield, check the label for the name of the wine importer. The next time you're buying wine, look for other wines imported by them—you may find that their taste preferences align with yours. If you want to purchase natural wines from abroad, find out which importers specialize in these wines; this will make it easier to spot them in a store.

For $15 to $20, you can buy good wine. For $20+, you can buy really good wine. But it's hard to find interesting wine for under $10 unless you stumble upon a buried treasure because someone is secretly trying to make it disappear. The best deals often come from regions that are less familiar to Americans but have long histories of making wine, such as Croatia, Hungary, and Chile.

Be open-minded about buying wines with screwcaps, synthetic corks, or crown caps (the kind you see on beer bottles). Canned wines are also moving beyond simple Prosecco, with serious winemakers trying out cans because of their lower environmental footprint and cost.

THOUGHTS ON GLASSWARE AND OPENING WINE

It happens all the time on TV: sophisticated characters reach for glasses of wine at a cocktail party, grabbing the bowl of the glass with their hands and forgetting the stem even exists. The horror! So to all the TV people out there, tell your sophisticated characters to hold the glass by the stem. It's there for a reason—to protect wine from the heat of our grubby paws.

With that disclaimer out of the way, if you're having a picnic or throwing a party with a bunch of fun glasses, serious wine tasting isn't the point, and please let your friends hold their wineglasses any way they want. But if you want to focus on the aroma and taste of a bottle you've been looking forward to opening, use a stemmed glass, ideally one large enough to let you swirl the wine. Although not absolutely essential, a thin rim allows the wine to flow to your tongue more easily. A set of plain, clear, stemmed glasses of decent quality works well for white, red, orange, rosé, and sparkling wines. Check the dimensions so they'll fit in your cabinet (some stemmed glassware is inexplicably enormous). Give away any champagne flutes—they make it hard to smell and taste sparkling wine, and those wines are special enough to deserve to be sipped out of real glasses.

CORKSCREWS AND OPENING WINE

The best way to open a wine bottle is with a tool called a waiter's friend: a corkscrew with a metal prong that helps you get leverage when you extract the cork. My favorite corkscrew was a gift from my friend Liz Hester, who got it while waiting tables years ago. I love it because it has a double-hinged prong, making it easy to extract corks. But use what works for you, even if it's the one that looks like a mustachioed man with arms that you press down to enable the cork to pop

out. Whatever you use, make it easier on yourself by trimming away the foil to below the lip of the bottle before plunging in the corkscrew. Trimming foil is also a good idea to check to see if a bottle has a glass stopper, which can be pried off with your hands. For wax corks, plunge the corkscrew right through the wax.

Sparkling wine is a little different. Some have crown caps, which you see on beer bottles and can be removed with a bottle opener (just be sure the bottle hasn't been shaken beforehand). When opening sparkling wine with a wire care, first put a kitchen towel around the top of the cork. Loosen the wire cage (or you can remove it entirely) and twist the bottle gently until the cork loosens enough that the pressure in the bottle forces it to pop out.

STORING OPEN BOTTLES OF WINE

There's no set amount of time that indicates when an open bottle of wine is past its prime for drinking. Some turn sour in a day, some last a week. Go by how the wine tastes to you. Stopper an open bottle with a cork and refrigerate to prolong the life of wine.

CHAMPAGNE STOPPERS

If you like sparkling wine but never drink it because you don't want to drink a whole bottle or open it only for one glass on a weeknight, a champagne stopper is just what you need. It locks in pressure so the wine doesn't go flat. Store the bottle in the refrigerator and it will be waiting for you at happy hour the next day. Don't worry if the bubbles are a bit different a day later—sometimes the less vigorous the bubbles, the more you can taste the wine.

KEEPING TRACK OF WHAT YOU LIKE

If you want to start connecting the dots between the wines you gravitate toward, find a way to record the names and descriptions of the ones you like. I can't tell you how many times I've taken a photo of a bottle to remember later—and then months go by and I've forgotten why I liked the wine. I've tried jotting down thoughts in a notebook for tasting notes, but the notebook ends up getting lost or filled up with shopping lists and the like. I could never keep it up. My solution? I started a very simple spreadsheet with columns for wine name, region, type (grape name or style), notes about what struck me about it, and an importer name if relevant. Now that I have a low-commitment place for my notes, I'm more likely to log information about a wine that I like or is completely new to me. Just the act of logging the information helps me remember it, even if I never look at the specific note again.

Your strategy doesn't have to be a spreadsheet or a journal. There are apps to help you track your wines, and everyone learns and retains information differently. Discover what works for you. The key things to note are the name of the producer, the name of the wine, the year it was made, the grapes used (if it's not clear from the name), and any notes that will help you remember what it tasted like. I also note the alcohol level, which signals the richness of the wine as well as how easily it pairs with food (a wine with 14 percent alcohol may need a meal with a little more heft than a wine with 12 percent alcohol).

Should I Age My Wine?

Say your friend is moving out of town and just offloaded a case of wine that was gathering dust in a coat closet for the past six years. Has the passage of time made the bottles more valuable? Probably not. Most wine sold to the public is meant to be consumed no more than three to five years from the date on the bottle, unless it's pricey and produced from grapes that are known to make wines that age, like Nebbiolo in Barolo or Pinot Noir in Burgundy. The majority of wines have been aged to some extent in a winery's cellar before being shipped to a retailer and then ending up in your hands. Some wines, such as Prosecco and Beaujolais Nouveau, are meant to be opened as soon as they're bottled because the whole point of these wines is their freshness, fruitiness, and easy-drinking nature. So while some wines do improve with time, most are good to go by the time they reach you. If you want to learn more about how flavors evolve as wines age, explore Rioja (see page 125).

Wine and Food

Some say drink what you like with the food you like. Others take a more strategic approach, pairing light wines with light food and rich wine with rich food. And some are all about contrasts, partnering wines with foods that are completely different to see if they clash or harmonize. All of these approaches work, and a lot has to do with how serious you really want to get (and since we're talking food and wine and not saving the world, interpret "serious" in the lightest way possible).

In the 1990s, food-and-wine media declared that it was okay to pair red wine with fish, and for many this was a revelation—red wine and salmon! Who knew? Yet we are still in the early stages of reshaping how to think about wine pairings, especially when it comes to the food of countries that don't have traditional wine cultures. Not long ago, I heard an explanation that the reason you don't pair wine with dishes from Thailand, India, Vietnam, Japan, Korea, China, and other Asian countries is that these meals are perfectly balanced at the table and don't need a beverage interfering with their culinary harmony. This implies two things: First, that it's not worth bothering with wine when eating some of the most vibrant food in the world. Second, that the classic dishes of Europe are flawed and need wine to complete them. Both of these conclusions are untrue. The real reason is that humans simply haven't been drinking wine with crunchy papaya salads, honeyed five-spice chicken, and coconut noodles for as long as we have with cassoulet and ragù. The same goes for the food of Mexico, South Africa, and other countries in the so-called New World of wine (see page 13), many of which actually have been making wine for at least a couple of centuries. Now that we're able to cook with ingredients from a much wider swath of the global pantry, it's time to experiment more with wine pairings at the table.

That's not to disregard the "what grows together, goes together" strategy, which I turn to when feeling stumped. The idea is that foods and wines that evolved together at the table are naturally complementary. Schnitzel and roasted potatoes with apples? A bright, white Grüner Veltliner from Austria does the trick. Any kind of pasta with tomato sauce is perfect with high-acid red wines from southern Italy, the home of San Marzano tomatoes. Olive trees and Syrah vines grow in the same place in southern France, and a classic flavor in Syrah happens to be black olive. Cheeses make the clearest case for the what-grows-together-goes-together theory since both fermented products have been important parts of local diets in Europe for centuries.

A few guiding questions:

IS THE FOOD ACIDIC?

Foods that are tangy and bright are best with wines that match the same level of acid intensity. For example, a salad dressed with a vinaigrette is a good match for lighter-style, bright wines, like Sauvignon Blanc. In contrast, a less-acidic wine, like Viognier, may taste flat or out of balance. Some high-acid dishes, like citrus salad, are challenging matches, even for wine experts, but a green salad with toasted nuts and goat cheese has the richness of cheese and nuts to counter some of the acidity from a vinaigrette. If the dish is light and spicy, a high-acid wine with a bit of sweetness helps add balance, like Chenin Blanc with shrimp seasoned with garlic and chiles. For tomato sauces, think about red wines that also have high levels of acidity, like Sangiovese. When looking for high-acid wines, watch for descriptions such as *bright, fresh,* or *zesty*.

IS IT SPICY?

The alcohol in wine makes spicy food taste spicier. High-alcohol, high-tannin wines, like Cabernet Sauvignon, can taste hot and harsh if a dish is strewed with chiles. Wines that are a little softer and lower in alcohol, whether red or white, don't interfere as much with the food's spiciness. A little sweetness can help, too. The trick is finding a wine that wraps around the spice level to tamp it down a few degrees. Pinot Blanc, Chenin Blanc, Riesling, Prosecco, pét nat, Gamay, or lighter-style Pinot Noir are all good options. If a pairing doesn't work with the spicy food, the wine can taste bitter or metallic on the finish. But if you love the burn of chiles, go for that big red and create a clash on purpose.

IS IT SALTY?

A lot of the same guidelines that apply to spicy foods hold true with salty foods. Salty snacks, like toasted peanuts, are good matches with juicy, round, and sunny wines that help mellow the salt. For more deeply savory or soy-based dishes, wines that are a bit restrained in both alcohol and fruit can taste more integrated. With Japanese dishes, minerally whites or reds work well, and orange wines can be especially good with sushi. Light Vinho Verde, which can almost taste a little salty, also matches up well.

IS IT FRIED?

If there's one thing that all wine people seem to agree on, it's the magic of sparkling wine and fried food. Champagne with fried chicken works for a reason: the bubbles seem to scrub your mouth clean and brighten the flavors of the food. This trick works for an endless combination of sparkling wine and fried snacks, from fries to tempura.

IS IT RICH BUT SUBTLE?

If the dish is earthy, like mushroom risotto, you can match it with an earthy, rich red wine. If it's buttery and rich, like butter-poached lobster, and you want to wallow in the decadence, you're still going to need a wine with acidity to perk up flavors, like a cool-climate Chardonnay. If it's buttery, rich, and casual, like a grilled ham-and-cheese sandwich, and you want a little contrast, turn to something bright with bubbles, such as Lambrusco.

IS IT SWEET?

Dessert with sweet wine is the most classic wine pairing of all time. Even before the advent of restaurant tasting menus with wine pairings, it wasn't all that unusual to drink a sweet wine with dessert. While you can drink sweet wine with savory food, it's not nearly as pleasant to drink not-sweet wine with sweet food. The best sweet wines awaken your senses and perk up even the simplest dessert of fresh fruit or biscotti. Just remember, drink sweet wine with sweet foods.

Cooking from This Book

A few notes about ingredients and other kitchen guidance when using the recipes in this book:

INGREDIENTS

Salt

Over time I've acquired all sorts of boxes and jars of salt for various purposes, from seasoning salads to mixing into cookie dough to sprinkling on juicy tomato slices. To be honest, it's overkill. For the recipes in this book, there's no need to invest in more salt than you need. These tips will help you make the best decisions. **Kosher Salt:** I prefer Diamond Crystal kosher salt, which is much lighter in texture and less salty than Morton kosher salt. If using Morton, reduce the amount of kosher salt called for in the recipes by 25 percent. **Flaky Salt:** For adding a delicate salty finish to a dish, use Maldon sea salt or other similar light and flaky salts that dissolve on your tongue and add crunch to the food. Flaky salt is less about seasoning a dish and more about giving it a light, salty finish. **Fine Sea Salt:** Fine sea salt, such as La Baleine, is great for popcorn because it adheres better to puffed kernels than kosher salt does. Most fine sea salt is twice as salty as Diamond Crystal kosher salt and a quarter more salty than Morton, so if fine sea salt is your main cooking salt of choice, reduce the salt in the recipes by 50 percent. You can always add more to taste later. The bottom line: If you want to keep your shopping list simple and your pantry inventory manageable, Diamond Crystal kosher salt is the best all-purpose option for all the recipes in this book, even if another type of salt is suggested.

Oil

Extra-Virgin Olive Oil: Out of all the other cooking fats in my kitchen, extra-virgin olive oil is the one I reach for most often. Its mild herbal flavor makes it an easy backdrop to wine, even in baking, where it curbs richness and makes recipes more inclusive to friends who avoid dairy products. Select an extra-virgin olive oil that you'd be happy to dip your bread into, and use it up within the year. (Olive oil doesn't age well.) For cooking, a consistent everyday extra-virgin olive oil, like California Olive Ranch or Bertolli, does the trick. For drizzling over salads or adding shine to food right before serving, consider spending more on an artisanal bottle from California or Italy. A green, cloudy olive oil pressed from the fall harvest will likely taste green and grassy, while deeply golden oils can indicate a more buttery, riper oil. The best way to find what you like is to taste different bottles now and again. **Other Oils:** Virgin coconut oil is solid at room temperature and has a lovely coconut aroma—choose it over refined coconut oil, which has been stripped of coconut flavor (stores like Trader Joe's carry both; just double-check the labels). Buy toasted sesame oil in smaller bottles and store in the refrigerator to keep it fresh. For neutral oils, any vegetable oil that you have on hand (such as canola) will work, though I like sunflower oil if given the choice. And if you've never used toasted sunflower oil, try it out. It's like toasted sesame oil but milder, and it's wonderful in dishes such as Beet and Potato Salad with Tarragon (page 131).

Spices and Seasonings

It's fun to pair wine with spices. Some pairings really work, others clash, but you always learn something in the process. Whole spices add texture and dimension, while ground spices and spice blends infuse more thoroughly into the dish. Buy ground spices in small amounts or, better still, grind whole spices yourself (a coffee grinder reserved for spices works great; clean it between uses by grinding up raw white rice). Whole spices, from cumin to coriander and fennel seeds, stay fresh longer than ground spices. A few more notes to consider when shopping for spices:

Curry Powder: Madras curry powder is my favorite curry powder blend. It's more savory and citrusy than others, although it can contain salt, so check the label and decrease the salt in the recipe slightly if concerned about overseasoning. Madras curry powder is sold in stores that stock Southeast Asian ingredients. Other curry powders vary tremendously in spice blends, so pick your favorite brand or buy a couple of them to taste and assess.

Paprika: I use paprika when I need a boost of color and a bit of red pepper flavor without adding heat. The kind I use the most is sweet paprika, though it's often simply labeled "paprika." The "sweet" descriptor doesn't mean it is sweet but rather that it isn't spicy (for that, turn to hot paprika). Smoked paprika, which is quite different, is generally not the best substitute for sweet paprika in this book. Though if you love smoked flavor, add it to the Roasted Chipotle Chicken Thighs (page 103) or the Toasted Rosemary Almonds (page 42).

Red Pepper Flakes: A fresh jar or packet has more spicy punch than older flakes, so adjust the quantity you use accordingly if you're sensitive to heat.

Black Pepper: There is more than one type of black pepper, and some are more fruit-forward than others. Spice companies such as Burlap & Barrel sell a few types of heirloom black peppercorns, so consider branching out and exploring the subtle variations. When using black pepper, I grind what I need with a pepper mill to ensure it's fresh and flavorful.

Herbs, Spices, and Seasonings: Dried and fresh herbs are used throughout the book. You can make your own dried oregano (or any other dried herb) by hanging a fresh bundle upside down for several days until the leaves are dry enough to crush with your hands. Before chopping or blending fresh herbs, wash and then dry them in a salad spinner or wrap them in a clean kitchen towel. If you have the space, place fresh herbs in a jar with water, cover with a plastic bag, and refrigerate for longer storage.

Porcini Powder: Porcini powder or a mushroom powder blend is made from dried ground mushrooms. Look for it in the spice aisle of grocery stores. (Trader Joe's calls it an umami seasoning blend.) Grocery stores also often sell dried mushrooms, which can be ground into a powder with a coffee grinder reserved for grinding spices. While I use mushroom powder in popcorn (either straight porcini or a mushroom blend), it's also great for seasoning steak and adding earthy depth to braises, ragùs, and roasted root vegetables.

Other Pantry Staples

Anchovies: Including anchovies in a dish isn't about adding fishy flavor—it's about adding savory depth (the same is true for fish sauce). When recipes in this book call for anchovies, you can opt for oil-packed anchovies, salt-packed anchovies, or anchovy paste from a tube. Soak salt-packed anchovies in water for 10 minutes to get rid of excess salt. For every anchovy fillet in a recipe, you can swap in ¼ teaspoon anchovy paste, though I always use at least ½ teaspoon paste.

Beans: Canned beans are all about convenience—mixed into a salad or pureed, they're an easy way to feed other people (and yourself) without a lot of time and planning. If you do have more time, dried beans can replace the canned beans called for in this book's recipes. One 15-ounce can of beans amounts to about ¾ cup uncooked dried beans, and two cans of beans is about 1½ cups dried beans. As long as you're going to the trouble to cook dried beans, I suggest starting with at least 1½ cups (leftover beans can be frozen in their cooking water). Soak the dried beans in water for at least 4 hours or overnight, then drain. Put the beans in a saucepan, cover with about 2 inches of water, and simmer until cooked through, 1 to 1½ hours, depending on the age of the beans.

Capers: I'm a big fan of the saline, oceanlike flavor that capers deliver. Alone, they can be crisped up in olive oil and sprinkled over roasted vegetables, but they're equally good chopped and mixed into dressings and mayonnaise as a seasoning. The most common capers you'll find are in brine; I suggest giving them a quick rinse before using to reduce the briny flavor.

If someone gives you a jar of salt-cured capers from a far-flung place, like the island of Pantelleria off the coast of Sicily, rejoice: they are truly special. To use them, rinse off the salt in a strainer, soak the capers in water for 5 minutes, then drain again so you can enjoy the floral, nuanced flavor.

Nuts: It's best to buy nuts close to when you plan to use them and store any extra in the freezer. Nuts have oils that can go rancid, especially walnuts, which have higher amounts of oil than almonds, hazelnuts, and the like. Toast any kind of nut at 350°F for 10 to 15 minutes, depending on the size and variety. To test if the nuts are ready, pierce one in the center with the tip of a paring knife; if the center is light golden, it's probably done. Better to err on the cautious side since nuts are expensive and very easy to burn. A friend of mine, chef Heidi Krahling, recommends leaving a nut next to your cutting board while they toast and setting a timer so you don't forget about them.

Olives: Buy olives you like to eat out of hand for any of the recipes in this book. To pit olives, press the flat side of a knife against the olive to flatten it—this will loosen the pit. Then use your fingers to pull out the pit. If it's stubborn, cut out the pit with the knife.

Pasta: There are so many good options for dried pasta, from durum-wheat spaghetti to gluten-free noodles good enough to please everyone, allergies or not. A few brands to look for: Rustichella d'Abruzzo is extruded using bronze dies, which give the surface of the pasta more texture. It costs slightly more than other brands but it's worth it, especially for Broccolini

Pasta (page 116). For rice-based pasta, the brand Jovial makes a variety of noodles and short pasta shapes that are chewy and hold up remarkably to serving cold, such as in A Really Good Pasta Salad (page 93). Brands like Barilla are also dependable, especially for spaghetti. For cooking pasta, add about 1 teaspoon kosher salt for every 3 cups water.

Vinegar: Inexpensive vinegars from the grocery store are much tamer and easier to use with wine than fancier bottles. I usually have a rotation of apple cider vinegar (like Bragg), unseasoned rice vinegar (like Marukan; avoid bottles labeled "seasoned," which contain salt and a sweetener, like sugar or corn syrup), and either a red or white wine vinegar or balsamic (Colavita and Bertolli are good everyday choices). If a vinegar seems too sharp for a recipe, dilute it with a bit of water. A pinch of sugar or a drizzle of honey can also help mellow the acidity.

Protein

Unless a recipe says otherwise, chicken is always bone-in and skin-on. In recipes for roasted chicken legs, pork loin roast, or tri-tip, seasoning the meat and refrigerating overnight before cooking will yield the most flavorful results. You can also season tofu with a pinch of salt for several minutes before cooking for deeper flavor.

Wine for Cooking

I never buy wine specifically for cooking, but I do save leftover wine in the refrigerator in case I need it for a recipe. Lighter, fruit-forward white, rosé, and red wines can be used nearly interchangeably, while richer red wines are best for making hearty, meaty braises or Bolognese sauces. However, if a wine has a lot of tannins and tastes bitter, cooking with it will concentrate the bitterness, so pass over these wines for recipes. A half-full bottle of wine stored in the refrigerator keeps for about 10 days for cooking purposes, even if it has lost its luster for drinking.

MORE COOKING AND BAKING STAPLES

Baking

While most of the recipes in this book don't include weight measurements, I added them to the baking recipes to make it easier to prepare if you have a kitchen scale. Generally, the way I measure 1 cup of unbleached all-purpose flour comes out to about 140 grams (I use King Arthur). To get the same weight with a cup measurement, use the scoop-and-sweep method: drag a measuring cup through the flour and level it off with a knife. (If you spoon the flour into the cup and then level it off, the cup measurement may be 10 to 15 grams lighter in weight.) For sugar, 1 cup of granulated (white) sugar is about 200 grams, and 1 cup of brown sugar is slightly under, about 195 grams.

Oven Temperatures

I roast a lot of vegetables and protein in a very hot oven because it's a simple way to extract a lot of flavor from everything from chicken legs to carrots and cauliflower. A convection oven is an even better way to roast because the air circulates, allowing vegetables to brown and caramelize more evenly without getting overly soft in the process. If your oven has a convection setting and you use it for these recipes, lower the temperature called for by 25°F. The cooking times may be slightly shorter depending on how hot your oven runs, so keep an eye on things.

Pots and Pans

Use the pots and pans you have on hand, with some common sense. Generally speaking, a large skillet is 12 inches across; and a medium skillet, 10 inches. A large saucepan holds 4 quarts or more, while a medium saucepan holds 2 or 3 quarts. If you're searing something like eggplant in what looks like a large skillet and the eggplant seems crowded, cook it in two batches instead of one so the food has a chance to cook evenly. If you have a Dutch oven that you use for everything, chances are it will work just fine in place of a skillet or a saucepan. Just use common sense: if a pot looks too big or too small for the job, it probably is.

Sheet Pans (Baking Sheets)

In many recipes, I call for a half-sheet pan, which is a 13 by 18-inch rimmed pan. It's the perfect size for roasting vegetables and meat and baking biscotti and flatbread. You can buy precut sheets of parchment paper designed for these pans from restaurant supply stores and online, making cleanup even easier. If you don't have a half-sheet pan, a sturdy baking pan used for baking cookies or a couple of quarter-sheet (9 by 13-inch) pans can work, too.

Recipes

SPARKLING WINES

POPCORN FOUR WAYS 40

TOASTED ROSEMARY ALMONDS 42

HARISSA DEVILED EGGS 45

CHILLED SMOKED SALMON SPAGHETTI
WITH CAPERS AND AVOCADO 46

SPICED CARROTS AND WALNUT SAUCE 49

All wines can be fun, but there's something about sparkling wines that makes people smile as soon as they're popped open. They're uplifting, effervescent, low in alcohol, and refreshing—and the very best are downright serious and special. Sparkling wines start out like other wines, but most of them go through a second fermentation, which is how they get their sparkle. Serve sparkling wines chilled. A quick way to cool down bottles is to plunge them into a bucket filled with ice and water.

TRADITIONAL OR CLASSIC METHOD

The "traditional method" (also called the "classic method") starts as grape juice fermented into wine like any other wine. Then it's often blended with other still wines, bottled, given a splash of wine mixed with yeast and sugar, and capped. During this second fermentation, bubbles form as the yeasts eat the sugar and give off carbon dioxide. Eventually, the dead yeast cells (called lees) are removed through a process called disgorgement (involving, among other things, freezing the neck of a bottle so a frozen plug of yeast can be removed). Before the cork seals up the bottle at the end, a tiny amount of sugar may be added, which is called the dosage. Before or after disgorgement, the bottle may be aged for quite some time before it's released, and the exact length of time and process varies quite a bit from maker to maker. Still, it's a labor-intensive and lengthy method, which is also one of the reasons wines made this way are so prized.

CHAMPAGNE

First, the basics: Champagne the wine is named after Champagne the place—a cool, sometimes rainy region in northeast France where sparkling wine has been made for centuries. A sparkling wine produced anywhere else, even with the same grapes and method, can't be called Champagne because French law restricts its name use. Instead, wines produced this way outside of the region are usually labeled "traditional method," "classic method," or "metodo classico."

Within Champagne, there is a lot of variety among wines. Some is made with Chardonnay (blanc de blancs—a white wine made from white grapes). Others use Pinot Noir and/or Pinot Meunier grapes (blanc de noirs—a white wine made with red grapes). A handful of other grapes are permitted, but few winemakers use them. Champagne starts out looking like white wine since the grape skins are removed before they can leave any color. Rosé Champagne is an exception: a little red wine is blended in for a pink color and slightly rounder flavor.

When buying Champagne, don't get hung up on whether it's nonvintage (blended from wines made in multiple years) or vintage (from a single year) or grower Champagne (wine made from grapes grown and bottled from a single estate). It's best to ask for guidance at a shop for a good but not-too-expensive bottle to get started. For the best value, skip famous brands with big marketing budgets or try out traditional-method wines made outside of Champagne.

CAVA

Spain's best-known sparkler is made in enormous quantities but still in the traditional method. Look for bottles that include a blend of local grapes, especially Xarel-lo. Cava ranges from everyday bubbles that age for nine months on the lees to Gran Reserva, which ages up to thirty-six months. They are nutty, citrusy wines, perfect for summery hangout sessions, though they can get more serious depending how long they've aged on those spent yeast cells. The best Cavas are possibly the best deals among traditional-method sparkling wine, though a new quality indicator, the Cava de Paraje Calificado (CPC), was created to recognize Cava's top vineyard land and differentiate it from the mass-produced bottles you find everywhere. Few bottles qualify for the CPC standard, and the ones that do are special-occasion wines.

CRÉMANT

In France, wines called Crémant, like Crémant du Jura, Crémant de Loire, and Crémant de Bourgogne, are made in the same method used in Champagne but often with different grapes, such as Chenin Blanc and Pinot Blanc. They're delightful and more affordable than Champagne. Be aware that some are slightly sweet.

FRANCIACORTA/TRENTO DOC

If a James Bond villain had a winery, it would be in Franciacorta, an area in Italy just east of Milan that takes French technique and pairs it with modern Italian style. While grapes have grown here since at least Roman times, Franciacorta reinvented itself in the 1960s with sparkling wines created to rival Champagne. Made with Chardonnay, Pinot Noir, and sometimes Pinot Blanc, the wines have verve, style, and prices to help pay for a Bond villain's lair. A couple hours east of Franciacorta, the Trento DOC is an even more established area for making traditional-method sparkling wine. There, French grapes have grown in mountain vineyards near the Dolomites for more than a century, and the area's cool climate and high altitude yields some of Italy's best sparkling wines.

ELSEWHERE

Making traditional-method sparkling wines involves quite a bit of time, space, and investment, which has been a barrier of entry for many. Still, there's never been more variations to try. Riesling sekt from Germany uses late-harvest Riesling wine as the dosage, the splash of sweetness added before bottling. In southern England, a warming climate is giving way to wines made with the same grapes and soils as in Champagne. There are also wines made with grapes that had never been considered for the traditional-method before, like Nerello Mascalese in Sicily and Voskehat in Armenia. The best part: we have a lot more bubbles to choose from at a range of prices.

Traditional-method sparklers are undeniably great food wines. They tend to have lean acidity and complexity, allowing the wines to stand up to fried food as well as fish, mushrooms, pork, sushi, and salty cured meats, like jamón Iberico.

Sparkling Wine Sweetness Scale

Some wines need a little sweetness to balance the flavors and allow you to taste more of the fruit. In the best cases, you're not even aware it's there. The European Union sets the following scale of sugar in sparkling wine, which you will most often find on the bottle. French terms are the norm, though some bottles may include the terms in Spanish, German, or Italian.

Brut nature, brut zéro, or non-dosé: Either no added sugar or no more than 3 grams per liter. If you weigh out 3 grams of sugar on a scale, this amounts to less than a teaspoon.
Extra Brut: 0 to 6 grams of sugar per liter
Brut: 0 to 12 grams of sugar per liter (this is the most common category for Champagne)
Extra Dry/Extra Sec: 12 to 17 grams of sugar per liter (this is the most common category for Prosecco, though it's worth seeking out brut and extra brut Prosecco Superiore DOCG)
Dry/Sec: 17 to 32 grams of sugar per liter
Demi-Sec: 32 to 50 grams of sugar per liter
Doux: more than 50 grams of sugar per liter (this category is pretty rare)

Bubbles and PSI

PSI—pounds per square inch, the same measurement for footballs and tires—is also the measurement for pressure within a bottle of sparkling wine. A higher number means more pressure in the bottle and a more forceful bubble. Wines with a gentler sparkle tend to be frizzante or pét nat styles, though it's becoming more fashionable for Champagne to have gentler bubbles to help people appreciate a wine's flavor. You can make sparkling wine cheaply by injecting still wine with CO_2 as if you were making soda water, and those wines likely fall on the high-PSI side of the spectrum.

Here's what to expect with bubbles

Tank Method (sparkling): 5 to 6 PSI (Lambrusco, Moscato d'Asti, Prosecco)
Traditional/Classic Method (sparkling): 5 to 6 PSI (Cava, Champagne, Franciacorta, some Sekt TrentoDOC)
Ancestral Method (semi-sparkling): 1 to 4 PSI (Col Fondo, Frizzante, some Lambrusco, Pét Nat)

TANK METHOD

This method is called everything from the tank method to the Charmat method, Martinotti method, Charmat-Martinotti method, or even metodo Italiano. The story goes that in the late nineteenth century, Italian enologist Federico Martinotti came up with the idea for tank-fermented sparkling wine, and French engineer Eugène Charmat perfected it. The process involves transferring still wine into an autoclave (a tank that can hold pressure) with a mix of sugar and yeast to start a second fermentation. As the yeasts eat the sugars and create CO_2, the autoclave traps everything inside so bubbles stay put in the wine. Once the fermentation is complete, the wine is given a small amount of wine and sugar depending on the desired sweetness category; and it's ready to be bottled. The method is not only used for Prosecco but also for a range of sparkling wines around the world.

PROSECCO

Prosecco is a fresh wine meant to be enjoyed as soon as you buy it. The wine was a breakaway hit starting in the early twentieth century when chemist Antonio Carpenè began using the tank method to make sparkling wine in Conegliano, a town in the heart of Italy's Prosecco-making area. Today, Conegliano sits at one end of the Conegliano-Valdobbiadene DOCG zone, a stretch of vineyards recognized by UNESCO as a World Heritage Site for grape cultivation. It amazes me that for only a bit more money than you'd spend on an everyday Prosecco, you can buy a bottle of Prosecco Superiore DOCG made from Glera grapes grown in some of the most valuable vineyard land in the world. The best Proseccos taste lovely and fresh, with gentle bubbles and notes of white peach and green apple. Because of its high acidity, Prosecco is charming with green vegetables and can hold its own with most seafood. It's good with cheese but will never supplant richer white wines in most pairings. Look for extra-brut or brut Prosecco for the leanest, least sweet options, though extra-dry (sweeter than extra-brut and brut) is the most common style sold.

LAMBRUSCO

Made from a family of grapes that fall under the umbrella name of Lambrusco, this wine was once made in the ancestral method, finishing fermentation in the bottle, until winemakers in Emilia-Romagna looked north to what winemakers were doing with Prosecco. When the tank method met Lambrusco, an export star was born—which is why for so many Americans, Lambrusco meant bubbly, cheap, sweet wine. But trends change, and now the wine is cool again, with its dry, refreshing bubbles that conjure violets and blackberries. It is also not always made using the tank method—some winemakers are going back to the wine's roots as a gently sparkling frizzante wine fermented in the bottle, like pét nat (see right). No matter the method, Lambrusco is a fun, low-alcohol wine that can be white, pink, or a deep, grapey purple. Drink it with everything from a few slices of prosciutto to a throw-down feast, like Thanksgiving.

SPUMANTE/ESPUMOSOS

Spumante is a catchall name for sparkling wines in Italy made using the tank method or the traditional method. In Spain, espumosos are like spumante: they mean a wine with bubbles, no matter what the method used to produce it.

ANCESTRAL METHOD

Centuries ago, these wines were often viewed as a mistake, created when a wine looked like it had finished fermenting and was bottled and stored, only to have the yeasts perk back up in warm weather and start to ferment again. Trapped inside, the CO_2 caused some bottles to burst under the pressure (glass technology wasn't ready for the sparkling wines we know today). Nowadays, these gently sparkling wines are made deliberately, capped with the same kind of bottle top you see on bottled beer.

PÉT NAT

Pétillant naturel means "naturally sparkling" in French, though wines made this way are also labeled "méthode ancestrale." Although it's a very old style of wine, pét nat is most associated with the natural wine movement and is now made all over the world. With those spent yeast cells staying in the bottle, the wines are often a little cloudy and vary in color from pale yellow to magenta. Pét nat is the definition of a picnic wine: juicy, bright, informal, maybe slightly sweet, and even a bit wild. In Italy, similar semi-sparkling wines are called frizzante.

COL FONDO

Col fondo is the Prosecco answer to pét nat, a way of making the wine before the tank method became so widespread in Italy. Since the wine is fermented in the bottle, it is slightly cloudy in appearance and a bit rounder in flavor, carrying the acidity and white peachy–ness of Prosecco but in a richer way. It's mostly made for locals, and many producers don't bother exporting it because (so they tell me) it can be hard to sell to people accustomed to clear Prosecco. But seek it out, especially if you're a fan of pét nat. Serve it with chilled shrimp, crudo, or even sashimi. If you make it to Venice or around those parts, ask for it in a bar.

POPCORN FOUR WAYS

The inside joke among sommeliers is that sparkling wine goes with every kind of food and popcorn goes with every kind of wine. While that is a bit of an oversimplification, what's true is that salty popcorn and refreshing sparklers make great company.

What kind of bubbles? That's where you can play around. Spiced and spicy flavors do well with sweetness, so popcorn with curry powder and lime zest is great with bright, slightly sweet wines, like Prosecco. Brown butter is phenomenal with Champagne because the wine's yeasty flavors love the butter's toasty richness. Garlic powder and butter give popcorn a savory accent that is perfect with easy-drinking Lambrusco. Mix and match these popcorns with still wines, too. Spiced popcorn is great friends with aromatic German and Alsatian white wines and juicy, picnic-style reds.

Popcorn

MAKES HEAPING 9 CUPS

---

2 tablespoons neutral oil (such as sunflower or canola)

½ cup popping corn

Popcorn seasoning (see facing page)

+ When making popcorn, I use a lightweight 4-quart pot that is easy to lift and shake while the popcorn pops. I've found that heavy cast-iron pots take too long to heat and cool, making it easy to scorch kernels, plus they're cumbersome to lift and shake.

In a lightweight large pot+ over medium-high heat, warm the oil. Add a few kernels of the popping corn, cover, and wait for the first pop. Once the corn starts to pop, add the remaining corn, cover, and shake the pot to coat the corn with the oil.

Lower the heat to medium and continue to cook, shaking the pot occasionally, until the corn stops popping, about 3 minutes.

Pour the popcorn into a serving bowl and mix in the selected seasoning. Serve immediately.

Curried Popcorn Seasoning

PROSECCO AND PÉT NAT

3 tablespoons virgin coconut oil

1 teaspoon grated lime or lemon zest

1 teaspoon curry powder

½ teaspoon fine sea salt

In a small saucepan over medium heat, melt the oil (alternatively, microwave the oil in a microwave-safe bowl until melted). Mix in the zest, curry powder, and salt. Pour over the popcorn and, when cool enough to handle, mix with your hands to coat.

Brown Butter–Porcini Popcorn Seasoning

CHAMPAGNE, CAVA, AND FRANCIACORTA

3 tablespoons unsalted butter

2 teaspoons porcini powder (see page 26)✦

½ teaspoon fine sea salt

In a small saucepan over medium heat, melt the butter and cook until the butter foams up and the edges start to brown, about 3 minutes. Remove the pan from the heat and stir in the porcini powder and salt. Pour over the popcorn and, when cool enough to handle, mix with your hands to coat.

✦ For a luxe alternative, skip the porcini powder and sea salt and add truffle salt to taste.

Spiced Popcorn Seasoning

PROSECCO, SPARKLING ROSÉ, AND SLIGHTLY FIZZY VINHO VERDE

3 tablespoons extra-virgin olive oil

1 teaspoon paprika

½ teaspoon garam masala✦

½ teaspoon fine sea salt

½ teaspoon granulated sugar

In a small saucepan over medium heat, warm the oil with the paprika and garam masala until aromatic, about 30 seconds. Remove the pan from the heat, stir in the salt and sugar, and let sit for 1 minute. Pour over the popcorn and, when cool enough to handle, mix with your hands to coat.

✦ Other spice blends, such as ras el hanout or baharat, can take the place of garam masala.

Garlic Bread Popcorn Seasoning

SPARKLING ROSÉ AND LAMBRUSCO

3 tablespoons unsalted butter

1 tablespoon nutritional yeast

1 teaspoon garlic powder

½ teaspoon fine sea salt

In a small saucepan over medium heat, melt the butter and cook until the butter foams up and the edges start to brown, about 3 minutes. Remove the pan from the heat and stir in the nutritional yeast, garlic powder, and salt. Pour over the popcorn and, when cool enough to handle, mix with your hands to coat.

TOASTED ROSEMARY ALMONDS

A bowl of toasted nuts is always welcome alongside classic-method sparkling wines, like Cava and Franciacorta, though the same could be said for everything from herbal rosés and lighter red wines to serious bottles of Nebbiolo and Chianti Classico. Because the oils in nuts go rancid easily, buying raw nuts and toasting them yourself ensures the best, freshest flavor. Almond skin adds a tiny bit of tannin, so if you prefer smoother pairings for milder white wines, opt for blanched (skinless) almonds and shave a minute or two off the baking time. Serve alongside cheese for a welcoming spread, too (see page 74).

MAKES 3 CUPS | CAVA, SPARKLING ROSÉ, AND FRANCIACORTA

---

3 cups raw almonds (about 1 pound)

2 tablespoons extra-virgin olive oil

½ teaspoon kosher salt

½ teaspoon paprika

2 sprigs rosemary

Preheat the oven to 350°F.

In a large bowl, mix together the almonds, oil, salt, and paprika to thoroughly coat. Mix in the rosemary (it's okay if some leaves fall off the stems), then spread the nuts and rosemary in an even layer on a half-sheet pan.

Toast, stirring the nuts about every 5 minutes, until slightly darker with a lightly toasted aroma, 14 to 17 minutes (if your oven runs hot, start checking for doneness at 10 minutes). To test how toasted the almonds are inside, pierce a nut with the tip of a paring knife. The center should be lightly tan but not white or dark. If the almonds need more time, toast for 2 minutes more and recheck. They will continue to cook when taken out of the oven, so it's better to err on the lighter side (trust me).

Let cool completely. Remove the rosemary stems but leave the leaves if you'd like. If the nuts look oily, don't worry; they will absorb the oil as they cool. Store in an airtight container at room temperature for up to 2 weeks. If you want to serve them warm, reheat for 1 to 2 minutes in a toaster oven at 400°F or toss in a sauté pan over medium heat for 1 to 2 minutes.

HARISSA DEVILED EGGS

Eggs can be tricky partners with wine, coating your tongue in a way that masks other flavors. But what nearly always will counter this effect is a glass of bubbles, which gently scrub your palate as you sip. Since the North African condiment harissa adds heat, a refreshing and low-alcohol pét nat or a Prosecco made in the col fondo style (see page 39) are great options, though you can never go wrong with a lean Champagne or Cava. I use a fork to mash the yolks for the deviled egg filling, though if you like a smooth, uniform filling, press the yolks through a fine-mesh sieve instead.

SERVES 6 | PÉT NAT AND PROSECCO

6 eggs*

⅓ cup mayonnaise

1 tablespoon harissa, plus more as needed

1 teaspoon fresh lemon juice

Kosher salt

A few pinches of paprika

Small sprigs dill for garnish (optional)

+ Use older eggs—fresh eggs often stick to the shells when hard-peeled. It's best to buy the eggs a week or so before you plan to cook them. Alternatively, use the instructions for hard-boiling eggs in an Instant Pot or other multi-cooker or pressure cooker—they'll be insanely easy to peel. Release the pressure right away and then remove the eggs and plunge them into the ice water.

Put the eggs in a pot and cover with water. Bring to a boil over high heat, then remove from the heat, cover, and let the eggs cook for 9 minutes. Meanwhile, fill a bowl halfway with ice water. Drain the eggs and plunge them into the ice water.

When the eggs are cool enough to handle, peel and halve lengthwise. Scoop the yolks into a medium bowl and put the whites on a plate. Using a fork, mash the yolks to break them up. Add the mayonnaise, harissa, lemon juice, and ¼ teaspoon salt. Taste, adding more salt or harissa if desired. (The deviled egg filling and egg-white halves can be stored in separate airtight containers in the refrigerator for up to 1 day.) Using a spoon, fill the egg-white halves evenly with the yolk mixture and top each with a sprinkle of paprika and a small dill sprig, if desired, before serving.

CHILLED SMOKED SALMON SPAGHETTI WITH CAPERS AND AVOCADO

There's something luxurious about having smoked salmon in the refrigerator waiting to be draped over bagels or avocado slices—or both. This chilled pasta dish, a tribute to chefs Hiro Sone and Lissa Doumani, takes smoked salmon in a new direction. From 1988 to 2018, the couple showcased their modern California cooking at Terra in St. Helena, California, a restaurant in the center of the Napa Valley. Hiro pulled inspiration from all over the world in ways that few chefs were doing in the valley. When I worked as a line cook at Terra, we often prepared a chilled angel hair pasta with smoked salmon, caviar, and a soy-caper-lemon vinaigrette. This rendition of the dish is perfect with brut rosé from California, Oregon, or France. The original recipe, in all its caviar glory, is in Hiro and Lissa's cookbook *Terra: Cooking from the Heart of Napa Valley.*

SERVES 2 TO 4 | SPARKLING ROSÉ AND CHAMPAGNE

---

6 tablespoons extra-virgin olive oil

2 tablespoons capers, drained and chopped

4 green onions, white and green parts, thinly sliced crosswise

2 teaspoons soy sauce or tamari

2 teaspoons rice vinegar

2 teaspoons fresh lemon juice, plus 1 lemon wedge

2 teaspoons honey

3 to 6 ounces sliced cold-smoked salmon*

1 avocado, slightly on the firm side

Kosher salt

12 ounces spaghetti**

Herb sprigs (such as dill, parsley, or chervil) for garnish

+ For a lighter dish, use 3 ounces of salmon. For a more substantial main meal, I recommend 6 ounces. I use cold-smoked salmon (pictured). Hot-smoked salmon has a different texture; if using, flake into bite-size pieces.

++ Gluten-free rice noodles from brands such as Jovial also work well in this dish.

In a medium skillet over medium-high heat, warm the oil until it shimmers. Add the capers and green onions and cook, stirring occasionally, until the onions start to soften, no more than 1 minute. Pour the contents of the pan into a small heatproof bowl and let sit for a few minutes. Stir in the soy sauce, vinegar, lemon juice, and honey. Set the vinaigrette aside.

Cut the salmon into ½-inch slices, trimming away any gray or brown bits. Cut the avocado in half lengthwise, remove the pit, and dice the flesh. Squeeze the lemon wedge over the pieces to prevent browning.

Bring a large pot of salted water to a boil over high heat and have a large bowl of ice water ready. Add the spaghetti to the pot and cook according to the package instructions until slightly past al dente. Drain the spaghetti and plunge it into the ice water, using your hands to mix the strands and ensure they get evenly chilled. Drain again and press to squeeze out any excess water.

Put the spaghetti in a serving bowl and stir in the vinaigrette to evenly coat. Gently mix in the avocado and lay the salmon on top. Sprinkle herb sprigs over the top and serve.

SPICED CARROTS AND WALNUT SAUCE

Lambrusco was the name of a sweet black Labrador retriever puppy I met at a winery north of Rome, so now when I think about Lambrusco the wine, I can't help but think of Lambrusco the dog. Lambrusco (the wine—though this could apply to the pup) is playful, cheery, and even a bit funky at times. But the sparkling wine (like the dog) performs for food, from salumi and cheeses to less-than-classic matches, like walnuts and spiced carrots. With some salty cheese, pickled beets, and bread, you have a complete vegetarian spread. For alternate pairings, try natural red wines from Abruzzo and Sicily. Go for wines that have some tannins to match those in the walnuts.

SERVES 2 TO 4 | LAMBRUSCO AND PÉT NAT

1½ cups raw walnuts

Kosher salt

1 garlic clove, coarsely chopped

¼ teaspoon freshly ground black pepper

4 tablespoons extra-virgin olive oil, plus more for drizzling

1 pound carrots, scrubbed, or peeled and halved if needed+

½ teaspoon paprika

¼ teaspoon ground cumin

¼ teaspoon coarsely crushed coriander seeds (optional)

¼ cup cilantro, chopped

A couple of lemon wedges

+ Skinny baby or teenage carrots are tender enough to roast whole and have thin skins, so scrubbing them with a clean sponge is enough to take away most of the skin (peeling them removes too much of the carrot). If the carrots are larger or the skin is thick, go ahead and peel them. Cut larger carrots in half lengthwise for this recipe so they roast and caramelize evenly. If the carrots are exceptionally long, consider cutting them in half crosswise so they're easier to serve.

Preheat the oven to 350°F.

Spread ½ cup of the walnuts on a half-sheet pan and toast until lightly toasted, 8 to 10 minutes. Once you can smell the nuts, they're probably done. Transfer to a bowl and keep the pan handy for the carrots. Increase the oven temperature to 425°F.

In a saucepan, bring 5 cups of water and a heaping 1 teaspoon salt to a boil over high heat and add the remaining 1 cup walnuts. Cook, stirring occasionally, until the walnuts soften on the edges, about 12 minutes. Reserve ¼ cup of the cooking water, then drain the walnuts.

In a food processor, combine the boiled walnuts, garlic, ¼ teaspoon salt, and the pepper and blend briefly. Add the reserved cooking water and puree until nearly smooth. With the processor running, drizzle in 3 tablespoons of the oil. Taste, adding more salt if needed. Set the sauce aside.

Put the carrots on the half-sheet pan and coat with the remaining 1 tablespoon oil, the paprika, cumin, coriander (if using), and ¼ teaspoon salt. Spread in an even layer and roast, stirring once or twice, until the carrots are evenly brown and charred in places, 25 to 30 minutes depending on their thickness.

Spread the walnut sauce across a platter and put the carrots on top. Sprinkle with the toasted walnuts, cilantro, and a drizzle of olive oil. Serve with lemon wedges.

CRISP WHITE WINES

BAKED FETA WITH OLIVES AND LEMON 54

SEA SALT CRACKERS 56

GREEN GODDESS VEG BOARD 59

OLIVE OIL BEANS WITH GREEN SAUCE 60

COCONUT CURRY WITH TOFU
AND BRAISING GREENS 61

GINGER CHICKEN SALAD 62

At their best, these wines are fresh, lean, and full of acidity, enough to make your mouth water. Think about the wine you want to drink with oysters or salty, tangy feta and olives. While light, crisp wines are perfect for summer, they also can be austere enough for fall and winter, perking up rich meals with brightness. Serve chilled, straight out of the fridge.

ALBARIÑO

Think sea salt and acid, just the thing for summer grilling season. Vegetables, squid, shrimp, white fish, or chicken cooked on the grill are all good matches for Albariño, the star of the Rías Baixas subregion in Galicia, Spain. At their best, these wines are crunchy and fresh, with a vibrant mouthwatering quality from the salty sea breezes and notes of citrus fruit. Beware of the mass-produced bottles, which can veer into bland Pinot Grigio territory. If you love Albariño, dig into other coastal white wines, like Vermentino from Liguria. And keep an eye out for wines made with other Spanish white grapes, like Godello, Viura, and Garnacha Blanca.

GRÜNER VELTLINER

Every couple of years, there's a wine that every sommelier falls for, and in the early 2000s, that happened to Grüner Veltliner. But like most love affairs, the passion for Grüner was too hot to last and eventually fizzled. In its wake, however, the trend exposed a bunch of us to this delightful Austrian wine. Don't let the umlaut misguide you into thinking it's going to be a sweet German wine: Grüner is mostly lean and green with lemon and black pepper notes (though some versions can be richer in body). Because of its acidity, Grüner can cut through the richness of schnitzel better than draft beer while also pairing well with foods that aren't always served with wine, from raw vegetables and dip to Southeast Asian curries. If you like Grüner, check out Friulano, the signature grape of the Friuli, a northeast region in Italy that was once part of the Austro-Hungarian Empire.

MUSCADET

Briny, with loads of acidity, this super-lean wine has for years been a classic pairing with oysters. Muscadet isn't the name of the grape used to make this wine (don't confuse it with aromatic and sometimes sweet Muscat/Moscato). Rather, the grape is Melon de Bourgogne, which grows in vineyards spanning the Loire Valley's Atlantic coastline. Along with "briny," words like "zesty" and "zippy" are common descriptors of Muscadet. Some bottles indicate "sur lie," meaning aged on the spent yeast cells, which suggests the wine may be a bit softer or even slightly sparkling compared to other Muscadets. The rare bottle may have even gone through malolactic fermentation, which changes the green apple kind of malic acid in wine into softer lactic acid. Even so, Muscadet is never a wine to pour when you're looking for something soft. This is a tart thirst-quencher, the thing to drink with chips and guacamole (if you're not already having it with oysters). If you like Muscadet, try Sancerre, a Sauvignon Blanc that is also from the Loire Valley, or Vinho Verde from Portugal.

PINOT BLANC/PINOT BIANCO

Pinot Blanc used to be one of the most important grapes in Champagne, though today it's more of an heirloom in the region. (Pinot Blanc is still important in Crémant d'Alsace, a traditional-method sparkling wine.) That's sort of been the story of this grape for the past century. Not forgotten—there's a lot of Pinot Blanc out there—but rarely the source of sommelier crushes. And that's okay! It might even be a good thing because it means that Pinot Blanc can be a not-too-expensive white for any occasion, with mild, green apple undertones and a roundness that makes it resemble Chardonnay's kid sister. (Even though I've included it in the crisp white wine chapter, some versions are round and rich.) When grown in mountainous areas, like Italy's Alto Adige, it becomes more intense and leaner, pairing green apple with flint, limestone, and even some citrus and herbal overtones. Give Pinot Blanc a chance—you'll either be happy with a mild-mannered white wine that fits the bill for a weeknight glass or you might find an underappreciated treasure. Try Pinot Blanc with everything from creamy, soft-ripened cheeses, like Camembert, to crunchy salads that have a bit of sweetness, like Ginger Chicken Salad (page 62). If you like Pinot Blanc but want something a bit more unfamiliar, seek out Edelzwicker, a wine made from a field blend of Alsatian grapes, sometimes including Pinot Blanc.

PINOT GRIGIO/PINOT GRIS

Through the success of marketing, a grape that was virtually unknown in the United States in the 1970s became one of the most recognizable wines ever.

Around the world, if you order a glass of Pinot Grigio, chances are you can anticipate how it's going to taste: fresh and neutral, like lemon water, but much more than that. Because of too much industrial wine being made to meet demand, Pinot Grigio became a wine that today is widely popular but not considered cool. Still, certain areas have winemakers who spend more time teasing out the pear, apple, and mineral notes that mark a good bottle. In Alsace and Oregon, Pinot Gris can be richer, creamier, and a bit more aromatic, with notes of orange blossoms, lemon curd, or spices. In Italy, look for Pinot Grigio from Alto Adige and Friuli-Venezia Giulia, two areas that succeed in getting mineral depth into their wines; some versions can be surprisingly rich. Because the skins of Pinot Grigio grapes have a copper-pinkish hue, some winemakers in Friuli-Venezia Giulia and Oregon make naturally pinkish-orange wines with the white variety. The acidity in good Pinot Grigio makes it easy to pair with food, especially antipasti spreads filled with sides of marinated beans, roasted peppers, and white anchovies. Eventually, Pinot Grigio will be less popular and more cool than it is today. In the meantime, take a chance on lean, minerally Assyrtiko and pink-skinned Moschofilero from Greece if you want to branch out.

RIESLING

I was confounded by Riesling for years because I never knew what to expect from a bottle. Would it be sweet? Too sweet? Not sweet at all? Then I learned, who cares? It's great no matter what! Riesling—the most important variety in German winemaking—is easy to like and can be the perfect thing to drink with a wide range of dishes. It's low in alcohol with mouthwatering acidity, whether dry or sweet. Some makers of Italy's famous Barolo wines have a soft spot for Riesling, growing it for selfish reasons—so they can drink it. In true Germanic attention-to-detail spirit, German Riesling is labeled by the ripeness levels of the grapes at harvest—Kabinett picked at the normal time, Spätlese picked later, Auslese from grapes even riper than Spätlese, and beyond. This sometimes, but not always, correlates with a wine's sweetness level, but the finished sweetness is really in the hands of the producer, so grape ripeness level isn't necessarily an accurate indicator of how sweet the wine will be. In recent years, there has been a shift toward dry Rieslings, which bear the word "Trocken" on the label. (There can even be such a thing as Auslese Trocken, which means very ripe grapes fermented dry.)

Riesling is also grown in Australia's Clare Valley, the Finger Lakes in New York State (the most notable American Riesling area), and pockets of Washington State, Oregon, and California. Oftentimes, American and Australian labels indicate if wine is dry or sweet. Be open-minded about sweeter Rieslings. With high-acid wines, sugar can function like salt, seasoning the wine in a way that draws out its other flavors. Sweeter Rieslings also help with spicier meals, ensuring alcohol doesn't fan the chile flames. In terms of texture, Riesling can feel like a rich white wine, but it delivers the kind of acidity that makes it taste light and crisp as well. It's this acidity and texture that make Riesling a great wine with cheeses. If you like Riesling, give Chenin Blanc a try, and look for a sekt, a sparkling style.

SAUVIGNON BLANC

The famous variety grows nearly everywhere and depending on where it's made and who's making it, the wine varies from lean and limey, full of green bell pepper and cut grass aromas, to tropical fruit salad. New Zealand is on the leanest end of the spectrum, while California falls on the juicy, fruity end. Somewhere in the middle is Sauvignon Blanc from the Loire Valley, most famously Sancerre and Pouilly-Fumé. No matter where it's made, the classic taste of Sauvignon Blanc is citrus, namely lemon, lime, and grapefruit. The wine has the kind of acidity that tames tricky foods, like vinaigrettes, and it's also a classic match with goat cheese. If you like Sauvignon Blanc, try Grüner Veltliner.

VINHO VERDE

This tart, citrusy wine from northwestern Portugal is crisp, straightforward, lightly fizzy, and very affordable thanks to high-volume production. In this guise, it's something you can drink all summer and leave it at that. But there's more to the story, and a new generation of makers is bottling even fresher, mouthwatering wines that are still a great value for their price (for now). Vinho Verde is named for the region where it's made, the rainy northern corner of Portugal, and it's typically crafted from a blend of local grapes; one of the most important being Alvarinho, the same grape called "Albariño" in Spain. Light in color and low in alcohol, Vinho Verde is ideal for lovers of crisp whites and is perfect with seafood, vegetables, and any kind of summer picnic spread. If you've already explored Vinho Verde, give Muscadet a try.

BAKED FETA WITH OLIVES AND LEMON

Years ago, I sampled a creamy Australian feta packed in a jar of olive oil infused with black peppercorns. That jar from Meredith Dairy demonstrated how feta—so often relegated to salads or garnishes—can turn into a standout in its own right. This recipe pulls inspiration from Meredith Dairy and combines feta with the classic Greek trifecta of oregano, olives, and lemon, gently baking everything all together. Served warm, the cheese is the perfect first bite with torn pieces of sourdough bread or Sea Salt Crackers (page 56). Feta's salty tang makes it a good fit with unpretentious acidic white wines. Sauvignon Blanc, Muscadet, or even a light-hued rosé from the Mediterranean all do the trick. Or follow the "what grows together, goes together" adage and pick a lively Greek white wine, such as Assyrtiko.

SERVES 3 OR 4 | SAUVIGNON BLANC AND MUSCADET

---

4 ounces feta cheese, drained of brine and cubed or broken into large chunks✦

⅓ cup mixed olives (such as Castelvetrano and Kalamata), pitted and halved or torn into pieces

3 thin lemon slices, seeded

¼ teaspoon dried oregano, or 2 to 3 small sprigs fresh oregano

¼ teaspoon coarsely crushed black peppercorns

3 tablespoons extra-virgin olive oil

Crusty bread for serving

✦ Greek feta keeps its shape a bit better when heated, while warmed French feta tends to be creamier and slightly more spreadable. Bulgarian feta is similar in tang and texture to Greek feta. Look for feta slabs packed in brine, which helps to preserve the cheese. The recipe also can be doubled easily to serve more people. If the package of feta you bought is 6 ounces, you can use an additional tablespoon of olive oil and keep the rest of the seasonings the same.

Preheat the oven to 400°F.

Scatter the cheese, olives, and lemon in a small heat-proof ceramic or glass baking dish (it should fit the cheese with just enough room for the other ingredients). Season with the oregano and pepper and pour the oil over the top to coat the ingredients.

Roast until the oil barely starts to bubble along the sides and the cheese feels soft, 12 to 15 minutes.

Serve warm or at room temperature with crusty bread (the cheese will firm up as it comes to room temperature). Leftovers can be stored in an airtight container in the refrigerator for up to 1 week; crumble spoonfuls into salads when cold or let it come to room temperature to scoop onto toast.

SEA SALT CRACKERS

If it's one of those days that calls for an emergency happy-hour session with friends, these crackers come in handy. The recipe is forgiving and offers the satisfaction that with just a little flour, water, salt, and olive oil, you can make something crunchy and delicious to eat with whatever you're drinking. Serve them alone, with Olive Oil Beans with Green Sauce (page 60), or with Baked Feta with Olives and Lemon (page 54).

SERVES 4 | ANY WINE

1 cup (140 g) all-purpose flour, plus more for dusting

⅓ cup plus 1 tablespoon (85 ml) room-temperature water

¼ teaspoon kosher salt

2 tablespoons extra-virgin olive oil

¼ teaspoon flaky sea salt

In a large bowl, mix the flour, water, and kosher salt together with your hands until a shaggy dough forms. Dust a work surface lightly with flour, then turn the dough out onto the surface and knead until it starts to come together, about 3 minutes. (Knead by pressing the heel of your hand into the dough and pushing the dough away from you, then dragging it back with your hand and repeating.) Return the dough to the bowl, cover with a kitchen towel, and let rest for 15 minutes so it will be easier to roll out. (This will also make it smoother.)

Preheat the oven to 475°F. Brush a half-sheet pan with 1 tablespoon of the oil.

Dust a work surface lightly with flour, put the dough on top, and pat into a rectangle. Dust a rolling pin with flour and roll out the dough into a thin rectangle large enough to cover the entire sheet pan. Try to roll it out in an evenly thin layer so it bakes evenly. If it springs back a lot as you roll it, let the dough rest for a few minutes before trying again. Drape the dough into the prepared pan, pressing it into the sides and corners as best you can. Brush the top evenly with the remaining 1 tablespoon oil and sprinkle with the flaky sea salt.

Bake until the top turns golden brown with blisters in places, about 10 minutes. If the edges are dark but the center looks pale and feels soft, break off the edges and put the pan back in the oven for 1 to 3 minutes more or until the center is baked through and crisp. Let cool completely on the pan. Once cool, the crackers should be easy to break into pieces. The crackers can be stored in an airtight container at room temperature for up to 5 days. If the crackers soften, toast them in a 400°F oven for about 2 minutes to re-crisp.

GREEN GODDESS VEG BOARD

At nearly every Easter celebration for as long as I can remember, my mom's contribution to the table was a platter of spring vegetables with a side of green goddess dressing. Before anyone lined up for the ham or buttery rolls, we'd dip carrots and radishes in the green herbal bath. It turns out that the same combination—an old-school California dressing and crisp vegetables—is also a great partner with lighter white wines. Sauvignon Blanc is an easy match here, and so is Grüner Veltliner, an Austrian wine that complements green vegetables. Tarragon and dill are signature herbs, but if you also happen to have fresh basil leaves or chervil sprigs, blend them in, too. If you only have tarragon, use no more than 2 tablespoons of fresh leaves or the flavor can dominate. Radishes, new potatoes, and other kinds of spring vegetables are perfect for dipping.

SERVES 4 TO 6 | SAUVIGNON BLANC AND GRÜNER VELTLINER

Green Goddess Dressing⁺

2 green onions, white and green parts, coarsely chopped

2 anchovy fillets or ½ teaspoon anchovy paste⁺⁺

1 tablespoon white or red wine vinegar

½ avocado, pitted and peeled

½ cup firmly packed fresh flat-leaf parsley leaves

¼ cup firmly packed mixed fresh herb leaves (pick at least two among tarragon, dill, basil, and chervil)

Kosher salt

2 tablespoons extra-virgin olive oil

½ cup buttermilk

Pinch of paprika or Aleppo pepper (optional)

1 pound baby potatoes, or larger potatoes halved or quartered

Kosher salt

1 bunch baby carrots (2 bunches if the carrots are exceptionally small), scrubbed clean

1 bunch radishes, halved or sliced if large

1 pound snap peas

To make the dressing: In a blender, combine the green onions, anchovies, vinegar, avocado, parsley, mixed herbs, and ¼ teaspoon salt and puree until blended but not entirely smooth. While the machine is running, drizzle in the oil, then blend in the buttermilk until smooth. Taste, adding more salt if desired. The dressing will taste more balanced an hour (or even a day) after blending because the flavors will have had a chance to meld. (Green goddess can be stored in an airtight container in the refrigerator for up to 1 week and is great as a salad dressing.) Taste and add more salt if needed. Transfer to a serving bowl and sprinkle with the paprika (if using).

Put the potatoes in a small pot and cover with 1 inch of water. Season with 1 teaspoon salt and bring to a boil over high heat. Lower the heat and simmer gently until the potatoes are tender when pierced with a knife, about 15 minutes. Drain and cool completely.

Arrange the potatoes, carrots, radishes, and snap peas in a colorful way on a platter and serve the dressing alongside.

⁺ To make the green goddess vegetarian, substitute 1 teaspoon white miso for the anchovy. To make it vegan, also omit the buttermilk and use a whole avocado.

⁺⁺ See page 28 about anchovies.

OLIVE OIL BEANS WITH GREEN SAUCE

I don't know why this was a surprise to me, but it turns out that white or speckled shelling beans are sneaky slam-dunk matches with wine. The decadent texture of beans in olive oil supports a range of more assertive flavors. It's as if all that talk of wine and cheese throughout the years should have been directed to wine and cheese *and beans*. This is especially the case for white wines with acidity, which balance out the creaminess of the beans. Look for bottles with a bit of a mineral or saline quality to complement the herb sauce on top. Coastal white wines from Corsica, Sardinia, Spain, Portugal, and Italy possess this quality. The beans are at their best when given time to soak up the onion, garlic, and olive oil, so consider mixing them a day ahead before topping them with the green sauce to serve. In the summer, serve with lush, ripe tomatoes.

SERVES 4 | ALBARIÑO, VERMENTINO, AND VINHO VERDE

Two 15-ounce cans cannellini beans or other small, creamy white beans, drained and rinsed*

2 tablespoons extra-virgin olive oil

¼ cup finely diced red onion

½ garlic clove, minced

½ teaspoon kosher salt

¼ teaspoon red pepper flakes

Green Sauce

½ cup packed fresh flat-leaf parsley leaves**

½ cup packed fresh cilantro leaves**

½ garlic clove, minced

Kosher salt

Pinch of red pepper flakes

¼ cup extra-virgin olive oil

1 teaspoon fresh lemon juice, plus more as needed

* Alternatively, see page 28 for cooking dried beans.

** Consider using a mix of herbs if you're short on parsley or cilantro or are not the biggest fan of either. Dill, basil, chervil, and chives can all be blended in. Just make sure you have a total of 1 cup herbs for the sauce.

Put the beans in a large bowl. In a small saucepan over medium heat, warm the oil. Add the onion and garlic and gently simmer until aromatic, up to 1 minute. The onion will still be a little raw. Pour the oil, onion, and garlic over the beans and gently mix. Stir in the salt and red pepper flakes.

To make the green sauce: In a food processor (a mini processor works best), combine the parsley, cilantro, garlic, ⅛ teaspoon salt, and the red pepper flakes and blend briefly. Add the oil and blend well, then mix in the lemon juice. Taste, adding more lemon juice or salt if needed. (Or chop the herbs finely and mix everything together in a bowl.)

Spoon the green sauce over the beans and serve.

COCONUT CURRY WITH TOFU AND BRAISING GREENS

This is a comfort-food kind of bowl made virtuous with handfuls of greens. A few years ago, I spent hours standing in the narrow kitchen of Burma Superstar in Oakland, California, documenting recipes for the restaurant's cookbook. The way the cooks built flavors with a few everyday ingredients became the method I adopted for making curries at home. This one is vegetarian, though you could stir in a splash of fish sauce for umami depth. Try slightly sweet Riesling or an extra-dry Prosecco, or pour a glass of Chenin Blanc, which nearly always hits the mark with Southeast Asian flavors.

SERVES 4 | RIESLING, EXTRA-DRY PROSECCO, AND CHENIN BLANC

3 tablespoons vegetable oil

1 medium yellow onion, finely diced

3 garlic cloves, minced (about 1 tablespoon)

1 tablespoon minced peeled fresh ginger

1 tablespoon paprika

½ teaspoon ground turmeric

Kosher salt

1 bunch green chard, stems thinly sliced and leaves cut into ribbons✦

1 large Yukon gold potato, cut into ½-inch cubes

One 13.5-ounce can coconut milk (full fat)

2½ cups water

12 to 14 ounces firm tofu, drained and cut into ½- to 1-inch pieces

1 teaspoon curry powder

½ teaspoon red pepper flakes, or 1 tablespoon minced serrano chile

1 cup cilantro sprigs, chopped

Chili garlic sauce or sriracha sauce for serving

Lime wedges for serving

✦ You can use 5 cups firmly packed baby spinach in place of the chard and stir it in right after the potato is cooked through.

In a small (about 4-quart) pot over medium-high heat, warm 2 tablespoons of the oil. Add the onion, turn the heat to medium-low, and cook gently, stirring often to prevent scorching, until the onion is soft and starting to turn golden around the edges, 6 to 8 minutes. Add the garlic, ginger, paprika, turmeric, and 1 teaspoon salt and stir for 30 seconds to draw out the spice aromas.

Add the chard and potato to the pot, increase the heat to medium-high, and stir until the greens wilt a bit, about 2 minutes. Pour in the coconut milk and water and bring to a boil over high heat. Lower the heat and simmer gently until the potato pieces are cooked through, 12 to 17 minutes.

Meanwhile, pat the tofu dry with paper towels, then season with a few pinches of salt. In a large nonstick skillet over medium-high heat, warm the remaining 1 tablespoon oil. Sear the tofu pieces on most sides until golden, about 4 minutes. Remove from the heat.

Add the tofu, curry powder, and red pepper flakes to the pot with the chard and potato. Bring to a simmer and cook for a few minutes to combine the flavors. If you have the time, remove from the heat and let the curry sit for 15 minutes to allow the flavors to meld even more before serving. Stir in the cilantro and serve with chili garlic sauce and lime wedges on the side.

GINGER CHICKEN SALAD

Burmese salads are some of the best in the world—they're crunchy, savory, and keep you coming back for seconds. This salad isn't quite Burmese, but it's inspired by the many salads I ate in Myanmar. Here, nuts and seeds bring texture, fish sauce adds savory flavor, and lime juice provides sourness. Slightly sweet pickled ginger brings the flavors together. An off-dry Riesling works well with the pickled ginger, while Grüner Veltliner and Sauvignon Blanc echo the citrus in the salad, reminding me of the salty lime sodas served in Southeast Asia.

If you have leftover roast chicken, shred 2 cups to make this salad. For a vegetarian version, swap out the chicken for chickpea fries (see page 85) cut into chunks or tofu as prepared in the coconut curry recipe (see page 61).

SERVES 2 TO 4 | RIESLING, GRÜNER VELTLINER, AND SAUVIGNON BLANC

---

2 boneless, skinless chicken breasts (6 to 8 ounces each), or 5 boneless, skinless chicken thighs (about 1 pound total)

¼ cup packed thinly sliced pickled ginger, plus 1 tablespoon pickling liquid

1 large shallot, thinly sliced or ⅓ cup thinly sliced red onion

1 small garlic clove, minced

2 tablespoons fresh lime juice

2 teaspoons fish sauce, plus more as needed

Pinch of red pepper flakes

Kosher salt

2 tablespoons vegetable oil

1 medium head romaine lettuce, sliced (about 6 cups), or 6 cups sliced little gem lettuce

¼ head green cabbage, shredded finely (about 2 cups)

Handful of mixed greens (optional)

4 radishes, thinly sliced

½ cup cilantro sprigs

¼ cup coarsely chopped roasted peanuts or toasted cashews

2 tablespoons toasted sunflower seeds (optional)

Put the chicken in a medium saucepan and add enough water to cover. Bring to a boil over high heat, then lower the heat and simmer gently until the chicken looks cooked through when pierced with the tip of a paring knife or when an instant-read thermometer inserted into the thickest part of the chicken reaches 165°F, 12 to 15 minutes. Remove from the heat and let sit in the cooking water for 10 minutes more, then drain. When the chicken is cool enough to handle, shred it into bite-size pieces with your hands. (You can do this up to 1 day ahead; store the chicken in an airtight container in the refrigerator.)

In a small bowl, mix together the ginger and ginger pickling liquid, shallot, garlic, lime juice, fish sauce, red pepper flakes, and a pinch of salt and let sit for 5 minutes. Stir in the oil to form a vinaigrette, then taste and season with more salt or fish sauce if desired.

In a serving bowl, mix together the lettuce, cabbage, mixed greens (if using), radishes, cilantro, and chicken with the vinaigrette and another pinch of salt. Sprinkle the peanuts and sunflower seeds (if using) on top to finish.

RICH WHITE WINES

QUICK-ISH PICKLES 68

WHITE WINE CHEESE BOARD 74

APPLE-GINGER PRESERVES 76

OVEN-ROASTED GRAPES 77

OIL-PACKED TUNA WITH POTATOES,
OLIVES, AND LEMON 79

ROASTED CHICKEN LEGS WITH LEMON,
RADISHES, AND CAPERS 80

The biggest difference between crisp white wines and the wines in this chapter is texture. Rich whites can coat your mouth a bit, allowing them to complement creamy sauces and richer dishes in a balanced, even-handed way. But the best rich food wines also offer enough acidity to perk up your palate. With smoked fish, roasted poultry, buttery shellfish, and a wide range of cheeses, it's hard to go wrong. Even braises, especially poultry or pork, can play well with richer styles of white wine. Before drinking, let these wines sit at room temperature for a few minutes after pulling them out of the fridge (between 50° and 58°F is the sweet spot). This way, you'll be able to better taste their nuanced aromas and flavors.

CHARDONNAY

If there's one white wine that just about everyone knows, it's Chardonnay. The classic grape has now been planted in almost every corner of the wine-growing planet because it cooperates, growing easily and allowing winemakers to put their stamp on it. That makes Chardonnay sound tragically unhip, but it also has made some pretty great wines. Chablis and blanc de blancs Champagne are Chardonnay wines, after all. The grape can reflect the land it grows in, echoing flinty or chalky soils with grace. The trouble with its popularity is that it's also fallen victim to plain-old bad winemaking, resulting in wines with shallow oaky flavor, flabbiness, or simply forgettable qualities.

Because the grape has been planted in so many places and is made in so many styles, Chardonnay can be lean or rich or somewhere in between. It shows off green apple, pear, and even lemon, especially if grown in cooler climates. When aged in oak barrels, it can pick up notes of vanilla and toasted nuts. Those same oaked Chardonnays often undergo malolactic fermentation, a process in which sharp malic acid (what you find in green apples) is transformed into mellower lactic acid. This rich, oaked style was all the rage until it wasn't. Then came the ABC club—people who say they'd drink "anything but Chardonnay." This is silly, though, because Chardonnay can be great! You just might need to do a little research before investing in a case of it. With food, wines somewhere on the lighter end or middle of the richness spectrum are generally best, though sometimes a rich, oaked Chardonnay from California can fit the mood. Butter-poached lobster, fresh corn, and Chardonnay? That's a classic flavor trifecta. Still, if you have had your fair share of Chardonnay, give Fiano from Italy a try.

CHENIN BLANC

In the 1970s, Chenin Blanc grew all over Northern California. It was the early years of California's modern wine era, and the Loire Valley transplant grew easily and yielded a lot of fruit, especially in warm, flat areas. But eventually, Chardonnay edged Chenin Blanc out of vineyards. For years, Clarksburg, a town in California's Central Valley along the Sacramento Delta, remained a sole Chenin Blanc holdout, a little-known California wine-growing area with an unfashionable grape. This is a lesson in why it pays to play the long game. These days, Chenin is all the rage, making delightful wines with Chardonnay-like body and Riesling-level acidity that every wine and food lover wants to drink. In the grape's original home in the

Loire Valley, it's made in every style from bone-dry to sweet and from light and low in alcohol to rich and almost oily (in a good way). A dream food-pairing wine, Chenin matches up with dishes from seemingly around the globe. Thanks to its acidity, it's also a great grape for sparkling wine, from traditional method to pét nat. Try Chenin Blanc with Southeast Asian curries since the wine can compete with the heat and aromatics of those dishes. Chenin can also complement rich fish, like salmon and rainbow trout. If you like Chenin, chances are you'll also enjoy Riesling.

GEWÜRZTRAMINER

This aromatic grape is not for everyone, but it has earned respect in wine history for being one of the oldest winemaking grapes in the world, the progenitor to Pinot Noir and Cabernet Franc. And its skins are actually pink, not green! For this reason, some argue it should be thought of more as a white wine made from a red grape. Gewürz means "seasoning" in German, and traminer comes from the name of the town of Tramin in Italy's northern Alto Adige region (which was once part of Austria). Yet today it's most associated with Alsace, which produces more exuberant, sometimes sweet, white wines. In the glass, the wine delivers notes of honeysuckle, lychee, and rose petal balanced with silky texture. Gewürztraminer is not a high-acid grape, though some natural winemakers are pushing its acidity levels further by crafting simple, juicy wines with the variety. Because of its lower acidity, the wine does best with rich foods that match those same acidity levels, like Alsatian tarte flambée (a buttery bacon and onion tart) or roast turkey with all the fixings. And because of

Gewürztraminer's subtle sweetness, it also pairs well with saltier ingredients, like soy sauce. If you love aromatic wines such as Gewürztraminer, try Viognier.

VIOGNIER

In the 1990s, when Chenin Blanc was patiently waiting for people to notice it, Californians were showering Viognier with praise. The result was a lot of heavy, rich, and overly perfumed Viognier made in a concentrated style borrowed from California Chardonnay. When wine fashion moved toward less exuberant wines, Viognier was left in the cold. Today, only winemakers who truly love Viognier are making wine with the honeyed, fruit-forward variety. When made well, these can be complex, nuanced wines, with honeysuckle aromas and layers of peach or pineapple. Viognier is from the Rhône Valley in southern France, where it's often blended with other Rhône white grapes: Marsanne, Roussanne, and a few other local varieties. Like Gewürztraminer, Viognier is best with richer foods without a lot of acidity to clash with it. You can't go wrong with roast chicken. If you like Viognier, ask a wine shop to recommend other Rhône-style whites. If you like aromatic wines in general, seek out Torrontés from Argentina.

ITALIAN WHITE WINES

For years, thanks to an export market that seemed to say Pinot Grigio or bust, Italy's best white wines were overlooked. Fortunately that's changing, but where to start? There are so many grapes! The following are some of Italy's most important whites on the richer side of the spectrum.

Fiano

Native to Campania, the region in southern Italy that is home to Naples, Fiano can be made in a range of styles, from light-bodied to expansive, but it's always graceful and grounded, evoking everything from chestnuts and herbs to orange blossoms and honey. It's more mineral-driven than fruity and grows best in volcanic soils. The grape was nearly forgotten about as late as the 1970s until local winemakers finally started to recognize its potential for great wine. (By the way, this is the story of many Italian grapes.)

Garganega

One of Italy's oldest and most valuable grapes, Garganega is known primarily as the main variety in Soave, a wine made around a village in the Veneto, a large region spreading from Venice to the foothills of the Dolomites. Some say the best Garganega wines mirror the best Chenin Blancs in complexity and nuance. Think almonds, citrus, and apples, all balanced by acidity.

Pecorino

Not to be confused with pecorino cheese, this grape from the Marche and Abruzzo regions, in central Italy, is named after the sheep that graze in the mountains. It's not clear if the vines were named after the grape clusters, which are shaped like a sheep's head, or because sheep liked to nibble on the bunches, or because the shepherds used this grape to make wine, and it doesn't matter all that much. As for the wine, Pecorino carries brightness but also richness, perfect for the first glass at the beginning of a feast. And yes, you can eat it with pecorino cheese.

Timorasso

Although the Piedmont region is justly famous for red wine, this white grape variety has become a star in recent years yielding rich, intense wines with high acidity and subtle notes of white flowers, stone fruit, and graphite. In an area best known for famous red wines, like Barolo and Barbaresco, a white grape has to be pretty special to get people to pay attention.

Verdicchio

The most important grape of the Marche region, Verdicchio may have arrived from the Veneto during a plague in the sixteenth century. It brings high acidity balanced by marzipan and green apple. When young, it's fresh and fruity though never super-aromatic. When older, it leans into mineral richness. I'm partial to Verdicchio di Matelica for the bright acidity the grapes get from the cooler vineyard area in the Apennines foothills.

Other Italian white wines to look for: Carricante (Etna Bianco), Falanghina, Greco di Tufo, Malvasia Istriana, Trebbiano Abruzzese, and Trebbiano Spoletino.

QUICK-ISH PICKLES

There's a misconception that making pickles involves sanitizing jars, taming a cauldron of boiling water, and mitigating the risk of botulism poisoning. But making small batches of pickles to store in the refrigerator is far less daunting. You can prepare these kinds of pickles when you have a bit of extra produce and want something bright and crunchy to serve alongside olives, cheese, and salumi. Here are the basics:

Find a clean glass jar that can get hot without cracking. I regularly use 2- to 4-cup mason jars or recycled jam jars.

Put the vegetables in the jar so they're snug but also have some room for liquid. Heat the brine on the stove until it simmers, then pour it over the vegetables. Let the pickles cool to room temperature, then screw the lid on the jar and store it in the refrigerator. I like to label them with the date as a reminder to use them within 3 months for the best flavor.

Carrot wedges, whole baby carrots, sliced red onion, and celery sticks can all be pickled this way. Beets are easiest to pickle if cooked beforehand. Cucumbers are best marinated briefly in brine and eaten the same day so they don't lose their crunchy texture. If you have leftover brine, save it for marinated cucumbers.

On their own, wine and pickles aren't easy pairings, but when both are part of a spread that includes cheeses, cured meats, and bread, they add balance and brightness to the table. Look for wines with high acidity levels so the sharpness of the pickles won't clash. High-acid wines often come from cooler climates or alpine regions, like Riesling from Germany and New York, Grüner Veltliner from Austria, and Pinot Noir from New Zealand. Unoaked Chardonnay, lower-alcohol wines, and many natural wines can be quite high in acid as well.

When serving pickles alongside wine, I tamp down the acidity of the pickling brine by adding water to ensure the pickles don't taste too sharp. A ratio of 1 cup water to 1 cup vinegar does the trick. Apple cider and unseasoned rice vinegars have softer acidity, though inexpensive red or white wine vinegars work well, too. (Skip expensive vinegars for pickling.) If you're not sure how much pickling brine you need, use this technique: Put the vegetables in the jar, pour enough water over the vegetables to cover them, then pour the water out into a liquid measuring cup. The amount of water in the measuring cup is the amount of brine you'll need.

Pickled Carrots*

MAKES 2 CUPS

4 medium carrots (or 1 bunch baby carrots), trimmed of greens and stringy root tips (8 to 10 ounces)

1 sprig dill or flat-leaf parsley

1 small garlic clove (optional)

¾ cup water

½ cup rice vinegar

1 tablespoon plus 1 teaspoon granulated sugar

1 teaspoon kosher salt

Pinch of red pepper flakes

Have a heatproof 2-cup jar and lid ready.

Peel and cut the carrots into sticks in a length that will fit in your jar. (If using baby carrots, scrub the skins with a clean sponge. Baby carrots tend to have thin skins, so they don't need to be peeled. Leave whole if they are very skinny and fit easily in the jar; otherwise, halve lengthwise.) Put them in the jar and nestle the dill and garlic clove (if using) along the side of the jar.

In a small saucepan, combine the water, vinegar, sugar, salt, and red pepper flakes and bring to a boil over high heat. Lower the heat and simmer, stirring occasionally, until the sugar and salt have dissolved, about 2 minutes. While the brine is still hot, pour it over the carrots (they will cook slightly in the hot brine). Let sit, uncovered, at room temperature until cool, then screw on the lid and store in the refrigerator for up to 3 months.

* The same brine for the carrots works well for celery stalks, sliced red onions, and radishes. Halve larger red radishes (or quarter if very large) through the root end. Watermelon radishes tend to be larger than red or French breakfast varieties, so slice them into thin rounds instead of wedges before pickling them.

Pickled Baby Beets

MAKES 2 CUPS

4 baby beets (or the smallest beets you can find), trimmed of greens and stringy root tips (about 8 ounces)*

½ bay leaf (optional)

½ cup water

½ cup apple cider vinegar or rice vinegar

1 tablespoon granulated sugar

1 teaspoon kosher salt

Have a heatproof 2-cup jar and lid ready.

Put the beets in a small pot, add enough cold water to cover by an inch, and bring to a boil over high heat. Lower the heat and simmer gently until the beets are almost tender when pierced with a fork, about 20 minutes. Drain. When the beets are cool enough to handle, use your fingers or a paring knife to remove the skins (do this while the beets are still warm or the skins will stick). Halve or quarter the beets through the root end, depending on how large they are and how easy it is to fit them in the jar. Put them in the jar and nestle the bay leaf (if using) along the side of the jar.

In a small saucepan, combine the ½ cup water, vinegar, sugar, and salt and bring to a boil over high heat. Lower the heat and simmer, stirring occasionally, until the sugar and salt have dissolved, about 2 minutes. While the brine is still hot, pour it over the beets. Let sit, uncovered, at room temperature until cool, then screw on the lid and store in the refrigerator for up to 3 months.

* Use any color beet you like. Red beets will turn your hands red when you peel off the skins, but it's temporary. When pickling red beets, save the pickling liquid to pickle red onions, which will take on a beautiful magenta shade. Baby beets vary in size, even in the same bunch. If one beet is much larger than the others, cut it into wedges that resemble the size of the other pieces. If baby beets are unavailable, use 1 or 2 larger beets. Simmer until cooked through, which can take as long as 1 hour, depending on the size.

Cheese and Wine

My friend Camille Fourmont, who owns the postage stamp–size wine shop La Buvette in Paris, feels it's always better to serve one really good cheese than a range of cheeses of varying quality. At her shop, she puts out one generous piece of creamy Brillat-Savarin and lets people dig in. When there isn't much to hide behind, the quality of the cheese matters, though buying cheese in Paris puts Camille at an enormous advantage. Still, all of us can make better cheese-buying decisions if we take the time to talk to someone behind a cheese counter or a cheese stand at a farmers' market. They will know how certain cheeses are tasting on any given day and can provide valuable guidance.

When you take the trouble to buy a good cheese, the goal with wine is to not let it get in the way. Wines with a lot of tannin—mostly red and orange—can overtake delicate cheese flavors, while white wines with high acidity, like Riesling or Chenin Blanc, are pleasant with a range of cheeses. If you want to get more precise, turn to the "what grows together, goes together" adage and pair cheeses and wines from the same regions.

Yet even then, there are learning opportunities. While visiting the region north of Venice that makes Prosecco Superiore, I met Emanuela Perenzin, who runs her family's dairy that makes the Italian alpine cheese Montasio. I sipped a glass of Prosecco with her cheese, but Emanuela wasn't satisfied with the match. She opened a bottle made with Manzoni Bianco, a hybrid grape variety created at the local enology school decades ago by crossing Riesling vines with Pinot Bianco. The wine was more perfumed and richer in texture, and though I was happy with Prosecco, Emanuela was right—the other wine harmonized better with the cheese. In other words, there is always something new to learn. Consider this list a starting point.

SPARKLING WINES
(the bubbles help scrub your palate)

Brillat-Savarin

Goat cheeses (fresh)

Parmigiano-Reggiano

CRISP WHITE WINES
(wines with bright acidity match the acidity in these cheeses)

Asiago (young)

Crescenza

Feta

Goat cheeses (especially soft-ripened)

Reblochon de Savoie

RICH WHITE WINES
(especially aromatic wines with decent viscosity)

Brie

Camembert

Comté

Fontina

Garrotxa

Gruyère

Mimolette (aged)

Montasio

Raclette

Washed-rind cheeses

ORANGE WINES

Aged hard cheeses (try the cheeses listed
under big red wines)

ROSÉ WINES
**(rosé wines pair well with many of the
same cheeses as crisp white wines)**

Caciocavallo

Feta

Freshly made mozzarella and burrata

Goat cheeses

Pecorino (young)

PICNIC TO REASONABLY SERIOUS RED WINES
**(avoid strong-flavored cheeses, which can overpower
wines such as Gamay and Pinot Noir)**

Asiago (aged)

Fontina

Goat cheeses (especially with Loire Cabernet Franc)

Gruyère

Raclette

Taleggio

Tomme/Toma

BIG RED WINES
(match big flavors with aged cheeses)

Cheddar

Dry Monterey Jack

Manchego

Parmigiano-Reggiano

Pecorino (aged)

SWEET WINES
With Sauternes and Tokaji

Brie

Camembert

Other buttery triple-crème cheeses
   (such as Mt. Tam)

With Banyuls, passito, port, and Sauternes

Gorgonzola

Roquefort

Semisoft tangy blue (such as Cashel Blue)

Stilton

Nondairy options: For those who avoid dairy
products or have friends and family who
prefer not to eat cheese, nondairy cheeses
have come a long way and can make a cheese
board more inclusive. Look for cheeses made
with nuts or ones that contain cultures, from
brands such as Kite Hill, Treeline, or Miyoko's
Creamery. Because these cheeses tend to
be more delicate in flavor, serve them with
lighter-style white wines.

WHITE WINE CHEESE BOARD

Presenting a beautiful cheese alone works just fine for some occasions, but for a picnic or other times when you want to serve people without any last-minute cooking to do, more options are welcome. Assemble an assortment that highlights the cheese but also leaves room for toasted nuts, fresh and dried fruit, and a few other options to eat with whatever you're drinking. When buying cheeses, estimate about two ounces of cheese per person, but err on offering generous portions over scrawny slivers. If you want to really get into a tasting of different wines with different cheeses, pick out a diverse selection—a sheep's milk cheese, a goat's milk cheese, and a cow's milk cheese, for instance. Or just ask a good cheesemonger for her favorites and purchase those—it will be hard to go wrong. With that in mind, think of this as less of a recipe and more of a blueprint.

SERVES 6 TO 8 | GEWÜRZTRAMINER, CHARDONNAY, AND RIESLING

1 to 3 cheeses, ranging from creamy to firm, at room temperature (go generous—it's better to have extra than to run out)

A bowl of Apple-Ginger Preserves (page 76)

Oven-Roasted Grapes (page 77)

Fresh and/or dried fruit (such as apricots or figs)

Toasted nuts (such as Toasted Rosemary Almonds, page 42)

Sea Salt Crackers (page 56) or crusty bread for serving

Set the cheeses on a board in such a way that it's easy to cut into them. Offer the apple-ginger preserves in a bowl with a spoon. Add the grapes, any other fruit, and nuts alongside to decorate the board, but make sure people aren't shy about eating them. Offer crackers alongside the board or slice up some bread. For larger loaves of bread, halve or quarter the slices so no one's holding a huge piece of bread. For sweet baguettes, let people tear off chunks if they'd like (sour baguettes have a harder crust, so it's better to slice them). Lay the bread alongside the cheese board or place in a basket before serving.

Apple-Ginger Preserves

This recipe yields a sweet-savory fruit jam, the kind of condiment that pairs just as easily with creamy cheeses as it does with roast pork or sausages. It's especially good to make for those of you lucky enough to have a prolific apple tree in the backyard and only so much use for apple butter or pie filling. I prefer using green or Fuji apples, but the preserves can be made with just about any variety firm enough to grate. Leave the skins on and use the medium holes on a box grater to grate the apples. If you have the time, refrigerate the grated apples with the sugar and other seasonings overnight to draw out the apple juices so the preserves will cook more evenly and in less time.

Apple-growing areas, such as Upstate New York, Washington State, Italy's northern Alto Adige region, and many parts of Germany and Austria, are often the types of places that make mineral-laced, high-acid white wines. Of course, it's not essential to drink a New York or German Riesling or an Alto Adige Traminer with these preserves, though I wouldn't turn down the offer.

MAKES ABOUT 2½ CUPS | GEWÜRZTRAMINER, CHARDONNAY, AND RIESLING

---

2 pounds apples (about 5), cored and grated (about 5 cups grated apples)

⅔ cup granulated sugar

½ cup apple cider vinegar

2 tablespoons grated peeled fresh ginger

¼ teaspoon freshly ground black pepper

1 tablespoon fresh lemon juice

Have a heatproof 4-cup jar and lid ready.

In a large bowl, mix together the apples, sugar, vinegar, ginger, and pepper. Let sit at room temperature for 1 hour or cover and refrigerate overnight.

Transfer the apple mixture to a large saucepan and bring to a boil over high heat. Turn the heat to medium-high and cook, stirring often with a wooden spoon, until the liquid has evaporated and the grated apple bits have softened, about 15 minutes. While stirring, use the spoon to press on the apples to break up the bits even more.

Stir in the lemon juice. If you prefer a smoother preserve, mash the apples with a potato masher to help break up the grated apple bits.

Transfer the preserves to the jar. Let sit, uncovered, at room temperature until cool, then screw on the lid. Label with the date and store in the refrigerator for up to 2 months.

Oven-Roasted Grapes

Have you ever packed grapes for lunch on a warm day and then felt less than thrilled about eating the lukewarm fruit? Drying the grapes in the oven helps prevent this because these grapes are best at room temperature. Pick up a cluster to nibble on with your cheese or save some to serve on top of the Caramelized Cabbage and Onion Galette (page 128).

SERVES 4 TO 8 | PICNIC-STYLE WHITE AND RED WINES

1 pound red seedless grapes, washed and dried

Preheat the oven to 350°F. Line a half-sheet pan with parchment paper or lightly oil it.

Cut the grapes into smallish clusters but keep them on the stems. Put the grapes in a single layer on the prepared pan.

Roast the grapes until they puff up a bit, with some juices caramelizing onto the parchment, about 30 minutes. Let cool on the pan and then serve at room temperature.

OIL-PACKED TUNA WITH POTATOES, OLIVES, AND LEMON

In Bacoli, an ancient suburb of Naples, the Di Meo family tends vineyards amid the ruins of a Roman aqueduct. I paid the family a visit to learn more about their La Sibilla wines, but I also received a lesson in southern Italian cooking, picking chicories from a patch next to the kitchen and then boiling potatoes and mixing them with olive oil while still warm. This all would become the base of a tuna salad that has upped my standards on all tuna salads. That afternoon they opened one of their wines made with Falanghina Flegrea, a native grape believed to be one of the oldest varieties in the region. With high acidity and a little richness in texture, it held up to the potatoes and olive oil–poached tuna. Local wine with local food—sometimes it's as simple as that. Beyond Italy, coastal Mediterranean whites and unoaked Chardonnay are also good options. Look for tasting notes that mention acidity and accents of lemon and honey; skip wines that are very floral or fruity.

SERVES 4 | ALBARIÑO OR CHARDONNAY

2 pounds yellow potatoes (such as Yukon gold), cut into large chunks

1 tablespoon kosher salt, plus 1 teaspoon

3 tablespoons extra-virgin olive oil, plus 1 teaspoon

1 large juicy tomato, diced

¼ cup black olives (preferably oil-cured), pitted and sliced

1 tablespoon fresh lemon juice, plus 2 teaspoons

One 4- to 6-ounce can or jar oil-packed tuna

⅛ teaspoon freshly ground black pepper

6 cups torn chicory leaves (such as escarole, castelfranco radicchio, or treviso) or romaine leaves

In a large pot, cover the potatoes with cold water and add the 1 tablespoon salt. Bring to a boil over high heat, then turn the heat to medium and cook until the potatoes can be pierced easily with a fork, 18 to 20 minutes.

Drain the potatoes and let sit until cool enough to handle but still warm. Transfer the potatoes to a large bowl and gently mix in the 3 tablespoons oil and ¾ teaspoon salt. (Mixing while the potatoes are still warm allows the starches to absorb more oil.) Let sit. When the potatoes are at room temperature, gently mix in the tomato, olives, and 1 tablespoon lemon juice.

Put the tuna in a small bowl and mix with the remaining ¼ teaspoon salt, 1 teaspoon of the lemon juice, and the pepper.

Put the chicories in a large serving bowl and mix with the remaining 1 teaspoon oil and 1 teaspoon lemon juice. Put the potatoes on the chicories and scatter the tuna on top and serve.

ROASTED CHICKEN LEGS WITH LEMON, RADISHES, AND CAPERS

Nearly every wine can be great with chicken depending on how you season the bird and what you're serving alongside. Deep-yellow, oaked Chardonnay can be tricky for pairings, but it's a perfect match with chicken roasted to the point that its skin is crisp and crackling. The richness of both the wine and the chicken are in unison. Instead of roasting a whole bird, this recipe uses whole legs (also called chicken leg quarters), which stay juicy throughout when cooked in a hot oven. Radishes and capers balance the chicken's richness with earthiness and salt, while arugula adds a peppery note. No-oak or neutral oak richer-style white wines also work, especially Verdicchio from Le Marche, a region in central Italy.

SERVES 4 | CHARDONNAY, VERDICCHIO, AND VIOGNIER

---

4 whole chicken legs, thighs and drumsticks attached (about 10 ounces each)

Kosher salt

¼ teaspoon freshly ground black pepper

2 lemons

2 tablespoons extra-virgin olive oil, plus ¼ cup

3 sprigs thyme, or ½ teaspoon dried thyme

1 bunch radishes, halved (or quartered if large)+

½ cup coarsely chopped fresh flat-leaf parsley

1 tablespoon capers, drained and chopped

1 small garlic clove, minced

1 teaspoon honey

4 cups loosely packed arugula or spinach

+ If the radishes have nice-looking fresh greens attached, leave some of them on so they can roast with the radishes.

++ You can season the chicken the day before roasting to allow the salt and pepper to sink into the meat more thoroughly. Refrigerate them overnight, preferably uncovered. Remove from the refrigerator 1 hour before roasting.

Season the chicken legs all over with 1¼ teaspoons salt and the pepper. Let the chicken sit at room temperature while the oven preheats.++

Preheat the oven to 450°F. Line a half-sheet pan with parchment paper.

Thinly slice 1 lemon crosswise, removing any seeds. In a small bowl, mix the lemon slices with 1 tablespoon of the oil, the thyme, and a pinch of salt. Arrange the lemon slices in a single layer on the prepared pan and put the chicken, skin-side up, on top so the chicken covers most of the lemon with some slices peeking out. Roast for 25 minutes.

Meanwhile, in a small bowl, mix together the radishes, 1 tablespoon of the oil, and a pinch of salt. After the chicken has roasted for 25 minutes, scatter the radishes around the chicken.

Roast until the chicken skin is crisp and the juices run clear when the chicken is pierced with a knife, 10 to 15 minutes more.

Cut the remaining lemon in half. In a small bowl, mix together the remaining ¼ cup oil, the parsley, capers, garlic, honey, and the juice of half the lemon. Season this sauce with more salt or lemon juice if desired.

Serve the chicken and radishes on arugula with the caper-parsley sauce on the side.

ORANGE WINES

ROASTED EDAMAME 84

OVEN-BAKED CHICKPEA FRIES
WITH TANGY DIP 85

KERALA-INSPIRED DAL 89

CUMIN-ROASTED CAULIFLOWER 90

A REALLY GOOD PASTA SALAD 93

First, let's address the name: Orange wine is also called skin-contact wine, skin-macerated wine, bianco macerato, and amber wine. Some hate the term "orange wine" because they say it's misleading—some wines made this way can be quite pale in color. But for simplicity's sake, we're calling this type of wine "orange." Serve orange wines as you would rich whites and light reds—a bit chilled but not fridge-cold (up to 60°F is fine).

HOW IT'S MADE

Orange wine is white wine made as if it were red. In regular white-wine production, grape juice spends as little time touching grape skins as possible before the juice starts to ferment. In red-wine production, the skins and juice macerate and ferment together for days or weeks. The end result is a darker, tannic juice. (With this in mind, red wine could also be called "skin-contact wine," though as far as I know, no one calls it that.) Yet while red wines are most often kept with their skins for two to three weeks at the most, orange wines can be stored with their skins for several months.

The technique of producing white wines like reds gives the resulting wines longevity so they are capable of aging, since tannins in the skins help preserve the wine. This method is most at home in the country of Georgia, the oldest uninterrupted winemaking region in the world. There, white wine is crafted the way it always has been, in clay qvevri—egg-shaped vessels that resemble amphoras. Slovenia, Croatia, the Czech Republic, and Friuli-Venezia Giulia in northeastern Italy also have a history of making white wines with this technique. The grapes used for orange wines vary by country, but favorite varieties include Ribolla-Gialla, Malvasia, Muscat/Moscato, Pinot Grigio/Pinot Gris, and Chinuri. There are also orange wines made from blends featuring everything from Chardonnay to Semillon and Pinot Blanc. The wines are aged in a variety of vessels, from amphoras to barrels.

Some orange wines are indeed orange, but some can be pale pink or deep amber. This comes down to the grape variety and the amount of time the juice spent with the skins. Instead of months, some orange wines sit with their skins for only a few days, yielding light-style, pale wines with bright acidity that can resemble unsweetened iced tea with lemon. More time with the skins translates (usually) into deeper color as well as more intense flavor and richer texture. These deeper, richer wines can taste like golden raisins or dried apricots while also carrying some bitterness. And some orange wines are in between, being tart but also slightly round, with notes of sour cherry.

The range is broad, and if you've never had orange wine before, start light before going to more intense wines. Or buy two bottles, one light orange and one more amber in color, and compare. Most orange wines are better with food, especially salty, savory dishes that can be hard to pair with wine. Soy sauce and sushi can match the savory quality in orange wines, while cumin seeds and other spices draw out sweetness and honey. If you like orange wine, try fino sherry from Spain and Vin Jaune from the Jura region in France.

ROASTED EDAMAME

Preparing edamame involves little beyond reaching for a bag in the freezer aisle, but the rewards more than outweigh the efforts. In Japan, boiled, salted edamame in their pods have long been a bar snack served with draft beer. I took that inspiration and made it for wine, roasting shelled edamame seasoned with soy sauce for umami depth. A light (in color and alcohol) orange wine is the wine equivalent of thirst-quenching draft beer, making it a good counterpoint for this savory snack. Or try something with a bit of fizz, like Lambrusco.

SERVES 4 (MAKES A HEAPING 1 CUP) | LIGHTER-HUED ORANGE WINE AND LAMBRUSCO

One 10- to 12-ounce package frozen shelled edamame

1 tablespoon extra-virgin olive oil

1 tablespoon soy sauce

1 tablespoon furikake or toasted sesame seeds*

* Furikake is a Japanese blend of nori, sesame seeds, and other savory seasonings that's sprinkled on everything from rice to Hawaiian poke. Look for it in the salt-and-spices sections of Asian markets such as H Mart, specialty grocers such as Trader Joe's, or other well-stocked grocery stores.

Preheat the oven to 425°F.

Put the edamame in a colander and run room-temperature tap water over to thaw slightly, then put them on a kitchen towel and pat thoroughly dry. Let the edamame continue to thaw as the oven preheats, then pat dry again before proceeding.

Spread the edamame out on a half-sheet pan and mix with the oil and soy sauce. Roast, stirring every 10 to 12 minutes, until the edamame have browned and crisped up in places, about 30 minutes. Sprinkle with the furikake and serve warm or at room temperature.

OVEN-BAKED CHICKPEA FRIES WITH TANGY DIP

If you know the Mediterranean chickpea flour snacks socca and panelle, this recipe is in the same ballpark but with a different origin story. Myanmar's Shan State is the main producer of laphet, fermented tea leaves served in tea leaf salad, a runaway hit in the San Francisco Bay Area. Apart from growing tea, the region also has a deep, resourceful culinary heritage, which includes making a style of tofu with chickpeas that is served cold in a salad or fried as a snack. I've borrowed the idea and simplified it to make these chickpea fries. They have a bit of bean-y funk that works well with skin-contact wines. The dip here is an alternative to ketchup—sweet, but not too sweet. Made with prunes, it echoes some of the dried-fruit flavor you find in many orange wines. This recipe makes more dip than you need, but leftovers work well as a sauce for pork, meatloaf, baked tofu, or chicken or pork Milanese.

SERVES 4 TO 6 | RICHER STYLE OF ORANGE WINE AND GAMAY

Chickpea Fries

1 cup (125 g) chickpea flour*

1 teaspoon kosher salt

½ teaspoon ground turmeric

½ teaspoon paprika

3 cups water

Tangy Dip

¼ cup pitted dried prunes

1 cup hot tap water

1 garlic clove, coarsely chopped

2 tablespoons ketchup

1 tablespoon fresh lemon juice

2 teaspoons soy sauce

1 teaspoon Dijon mustard

1 teaspoon honey

¼ teaspoon ground allspice

1 tablespoon vegetable oil

Flaky sea salt

* Look for chickpea flour (also called garbanzo bean flour) in the bulk bins of grocery stores and in the gluten-free section in the baking aisle. You can also find it in Indian grocery stores, where it's called besan.

To make the chickpea fries: Lightly oil an 8-inch square baking dish.

In a medium bowl, whisk together the flour, kosher salt, turmeric, paprika, and 1 cup of the water until smooth and lump-free. Let sit for 10 minutes to hydrate.

Scrape the batter into a saucepan and whisk in the remaining 2 cups water. Bring the batter to a simmer over medium-high heat, whisking to break up any lumps. Lower the heat and simmer gently, stirring constantly with a wooden spoon, until the batter has thickened to the consistency of a very thick hot cereal and leaves a thin film of batter at the bottom of the pot, 6 to 8 minutes.

Pour the batter into the prepared baking dish and smooth out the top with the back of a dampened spoon or offset spatula. Let cool at room temperature until set, about 1 hour (alternatively, refrigerate for 30 minutes). When ready, it will spring back slightly when pressed but feel firm enough to slice.

CONTINUED

OVEN-BAKED CHICKPEA FRIES
WITH TANGY DIP, CONTINUED

To make the dip: In a small bowl, combine the prunes and hot tap water and soak for 10 minutes; drain the prunes, saving ½ cup of the soaking water. In a food processor or blender, combine the prunes, reserved soaking water, garlic, ketchup, lemon juice, soy sauce, mustard, honey, and allspice and blend until smooth.

Preheat the oven to 450°F. Line a half-sheet pan with parchment paper or aluminum foil (the fries tend to stick to unlined pans, even if oiled).

Unmold the chickpea cake onto a cutting board. Cut in half, then cut each half crosswise into 7 pieces to make a total of 14 "fries." Arrange the fries on the prepared pan. Brush on all sides with the oil, then sprinkle with flaky sea salt. Bake until the tops are golden, about 15 minutes. Serve warm with the dip on the side.

KERALA-INSPIRED DAL

In the recipe for Olive Oil Beans with Green Sauce (page 60), I mention that beans are great matches with wine, though often overlooked. The same is true with lentils. Dal, an everyday dish of simmered lentils made in countless ways across India and the diaspora, is especially good with orange wines. While big red wines can overwhelm lentils, orange wines complement the savory and spiced flavors in a near-seamless way. This simple, warming dal is inspired by Kerala, a state on the southwestern coast of India known for its spice farms and trellised tea-growing areas. When I visited, nearly every version I ate included black mustard seeds fried in coconut oil, cumin and coriander seeds, a handful of curry leaves, and a dried red pepper or two. I've adapted this version over the years to what I have on hand, but someday I'll return to taste the original. Serve the dal spooned over rice with a lighter-hued, slightly chilled orange wine. If that is out of reach, a leaner-bodied Chenin Blanc brings a nice dose of acidity to the table.

SERVES 4 | LIGHTER-HUED ORANGE WINES
AND CHENIN BLANC

---

1 cup red lentils

3½ cups water, plus more as needed

Kosher salt

½ teaspoon paprika

Heaping ¼ teaspoon ground turmeric

¼ teaspoon red pepper flakes, plus more for garnish (optional)

2 tablespoons virgin coconut oil or vegetable oil

¼ teaspoon black mustard seeds

½ teaspoon coriander seeds, coarsely crushed (optional)✦

¼ teaspoon cumin seeds

½ medium yellow or red onion, finely diced

3 garlic cloves, minced (about 1 tablespoon)

1 tablespoon minced peeled fresh ginger

¼ cup coarsely chopped fresh cilantro leaves, plus more for garnish (optional)

1 lemon or lime, cut into wedges

Plain whole milk yogurt for garnish (optional)

Steamed rice for serving

In a medium saucepan, stir together the lentils, water, ½ teaspoon salt, paprika, turmeric, and red pepper flakes and bring to a boil over high heat. Lower the heat and simmer gently until the lentils have absorbed most of the water, 12 to 15 minutes. Taste a few lentils; if they are still firm in the center, add another ¼ cup water at a time and continue to cook until they are completely soft.

In a medium skillet over medium-high heat, melt the coconut oil. Add the mustard seeds and fry until they begin to pop and smell a bit like popcorn, about 1 minute. Quickly add the coriander (if using), cumin, onion, garlic, and ginger, and turn the heat to medium to avoid burning the spices. Cook, stirring occasionally, until the onion starts to soften, 1 to 2 minutes, then scrape the onion mixture into the pan with the lentils and give everything a good stir. Mix in the cilantro and a squeeze of lemon and taste, adding more salt if desired. If you have the time, let this dal sit for 30 minutes or longer to let the flavors come together.

Bring the dal to a simmer. Taste, adding more lemon juice or salt if desired. Spoon the dal into a bowl, garnish with yogurt, red pepper flakes, and/or cilantro, if desired, and serve with rice.

✦ To crush coriander seeds, put them on a cutting board and press a pan on top.

CUMIN-ROASTED CAULIFLOWER

Cumin seeds, with their earthy flavors and underlying sweetness, are a slam-dunk match with skin-contact wines. Adding vinegar-soaked raisins to the cauliflower as it roasts makes this side dish perfect for deeper-hued styles of orange wine, which typically have had longer contact with grape skins and coat your mouth a bit more than light-colored orange wines. Crushed coriander seeds—if you have them handy—bring an amazing orange-blossom aroma to the table, though they are not essential. Serve the cauliflower on its own as a side or a snack or with dal (see page 89) for a full meal. For an alternative wine, try aromatic Gewürztraminer, which can play up the sweetness of the roasted cauliflower.

SERVES 4 | DEEPER-HUED ORANGE WINE AND GEWÜRZTRAMINER

1 medium head cauliflower, cut into florets (about 6 cups)

3 tablespoons extra-virgin olive oil, plus 1 teaspoon

½ teaspoon kosher salt

½ teaspoon cumin seeds

½ teaspoon coriander seeds, coarsely crushed (see note, page 89; optional)

¼ medium red or yellow onion, thinly sliced

¼ cup raisins, chopped

1 tablespoon red wine vinegar

¼ cup firmly packed fresh cilantro leaves, coarsely chopped

Flaky sea salt (optional)

Preheat the oven to 450°F.✦ Line a half-sheet pan with parchment paper for easier clean-up, though it is not essential.

If any of the cauliflower florets are quite large, halve them so the pieces are similar in size. Place them in a large bowl; add the 3 tablespoons oil, the kosher salt, cumin, and coriander (if using); and thoroughly mix together using your hands. Spread the cauliflower out in an even layer on the prepared pan. Roast until the cauliflower starts to soften and has browned around the edges, about 15 minutes.

Meanwhile, in a small bowl, mix together the onion, raisins, vinegar, and remaining 1 teaspoon oil.

After the cauliflower has roasted for 15 minutes, remove the pan from the oven and add the onion-raisin mixture, stirring it into the cauliflower. Roast until the raisins are a little crispy and the onion and cauliflower are tender and slightly charred in places, 6 to 10 minutes more.

Sprinkle the cilantro over the top and season with flaky sea salt, if desired. Serve immediately.

✦ If you have a convection setting on your oven, I highly encourage you to use it when roasting the cauliflower because it will caramelize faster and more evenly. Set the oven at 425°F convection and monitor the final minutes for browning, since the cauliflower will brown faster this way.

A REALLY GOOD PASTA SALAD

We've all had bad pasta salad, the kind that cries out for vinegar and salt. But pasta salads persist because they are handy for lunch, picnics, and dinners on hot nights—and they can be really good! The key is a vinaigrette that holds its own even when refrigerated. That's why this particular pasta salad is a favorite of mine. Soy sauce and sesame oil boost depth, while arugula gives it a peppery accent. The combo of soy sauce and green onions stands up to richer orange wines, which can handle the concentrated salty flavors of the vinaigrette. Though no one would complain if you poured them a glass of lightly chilled Gamay instead.

SERVES 4 TO 6 | MEDIUM TO RICH ORANGE WINE AND GAMAY

---

2 boneless, skinless chicken breasts (6 to 8 ounces each), or 5 boneless, skinless chicken thighs (about 1 pound total)

⅓ cup vegetable oil

1 tablespoon toasted sesame oil

¼ cup red wine vinegar

¼ cup soy sauce

4 green onions, white and green parts, thinly sliced

1 tablespoon grated peeled fresh ginger

1 tablespoon honey

¼ teaspoon red pepper flakes✦

12 ounces short pasta (such as rigatoni, fusilli, penne, or radiatore)

3 cups loosely packed baby spinach✦✦

3 cups loosely packed arugula

Flaky sea salt (optional)

✦ For less heat, serve the red pepper on the side.

✦✦ The total amount of greens needed for this recipe is 6 cups (about 5 ounces). If you have more spinach than arugula or want to use solely one or the other, just make sure you have about 6 cups.

Put the chicken in a medium saucepan and add enough water to cover. Bring to a boil over high heat, then lower the heat and simmer gently until the chicken looks cooked through when pierced with the tip of a paring knife or when an instant-read thermometer inserted into the thickest part of the chicken reaches 165°F, 12 to 15 minutes. Remove from the heat and let sit in the cooking water for 10 minutes more, then drain the chicken. When the chicken is cool enough to handle, shred it into bite-size pieces with your hands. (You can do this 1 day ahead; store the chicken in an airtight container in the refrigerator.)

In a jar, combine both oils, the vinegar, soy sauce, green onions, ginger, honey, and red pepper flakes and give this vinaigrette a good shake.

Meanwhile, bring a large pot of salted water to a boil over high heat. Add the pasta and cook according to the package instructions until al dente. Drain and rinse briefly with cold water, stirring with a wooden spoon so the pasta doesn't stick together. Drain well, then transfer to a large bowl.

Add the chicken and vinaigrette to the pasta and mix well until everything is coated. Cover and refrigerate for at least 2 hours or overnight. Before serving, mix in the spinach and arugula. Taste, sprinkling with a little flaky sea salt, if desired. Leftover pasta salad keeps in the refrigerator for up to 5 days.

ROSÉ WINES

GOAT CHEESE WITH ALMONDS
AND DRIED CHERRIES 96

ROASTED SQUASH WEDGES 99

POACHED SALMON WITH FENNEL-CELERY
SALAD AND CAPER MAYO 100

ROASTED CHIPOTLE CHICKEN THIGHS 103

LAMB MEATBALLS WITH YOGURT SAUCE 104

When ranking the easiest wines in the world to love, it's impossible to leave rosé off the list. Unpretentious and easy to find, rosé (rosado in Spanish and rosato in Italian) is often the perfect food wine, filled with bright, tart red-fruit flavors. Serve rosés as you would crisp whites—right out of the fridge.

HOW IT'S MADE

If orange wine is a white wine made like a red, rosé is a red wine made *almost* like a white, meaning all fruit and acidity with mostly no bitterness. There are three main ways to make rosé. The most common involves crushing red grapes and leaving the juices and skins together just enough to extract color but not so long as to draw out bitterness. The juice is then separated from the skins, and finally fermented. For the very pale, celebrated rosé made in Provence, whole clusters of grapes are pressed very slowly so the skins barely impart any color before the juice is whisked away. There's also the saignée method, which literally means "a bleeding" but isn't nearly as gruesome as it sounds. Visualize a heap of red grapes crushed under their own weight. The first juice to run off is separated and turned into rosé, while the remaining becomes red wine. The third and cheapest way to make rosé is by mixing red and white wines together to get the pink shade.

Light, crisp Provençal rosé, with its subtle notes of the Mediterranean, define a French Riviera summer, though great rosé is now made around the world, ranging in color from the lightest pink to the deepest, translucent cherry. They are usually young wines, though some age well (and cost a lot more than most bottles).

Like orange wines, rosé is made with any number of grapes. In Provence, the classic varieties include Cinsault, Grenache, Syrah, and Mourvèdre, and many rosé makers use similar grapes. Tavel rosé is a deeper-hued, richer wine from the southern Rhône, made with the same grapes. In Spain, rosado is crafted with local grapes, from Garnacha (a synonym of Grenache, see page 123) to Tempranillo and many others. Spain also makes clarete, which is either a deep rosado or a light red wine, depending on how you want to spin it.

In Italy, rosato wines are produced just about everywhere, but they're mostly known in Abruzzo for Cerasuolo d'Abruzzo (see Montepulciano page 108) and around Lake Garda in the north, which makes Chiaretto. In California, some of the best rosé is made with Grenache, while in Oregon and New Zealand, look for lovely renditions made with Pinot Noir. If you like the freshness of rosé, try crisp white wines, like Sauvignon Blanc, Pinot Gris/Grigio, and Vermentino. If you like the fruit-forward side of rosé, try red wines made with Montepulciano or Grenache grapes.

GOAT CHEESE WITH ALMONDS AND DRIED CHERRIES

Some of my favorite rosés are bright, lean, and evocative of summertime cherries, from sour varieties to deep-red Bings. Fresh goat cheese is a tried-and-true match with pale Provençal-style rosés because the acidity in the cheese aligns with that in the wines. In this recipe, dried cherries soaked in a bit of vinegar dress up fresh goat cheese in a thoughtful way that furthers the flavor parallels between the cheese and wine. I like sour Montmorency cherries, though any dried cherries you can find will do the trick. Dried cranberries also work in a pinch.

SERVES 3 OR 4 | LIGHT ROSÉ

¼ cup dried cherries, preferably unsweetened

2 tablespoons red or white wine vinegar

4 ounces fresh goat cheese (chèvre), at room temperature

1 tablespoon minced red onion

1 tablespoon extra-virgin olive oil

1 teaspoon fresh lemon juice

¼ cup toasted almonds (such as Toasted Rosemary Almonds, page 42), coarsely chopped

Freshly ground black pepper

Sea Salt Crackers (page 56) or crusty bread for serving

In a small bowl, soak the cherries in the vinegar and enough hot tap water to cover until they plump up, about 10 minutes. Drain.

Crumble the goat cheese into a medium bowl and add the onion, oil, and lemon juice. Using a rubber spatula, mix the cheese and seasonings together until evenly dispersed. Transfer to a serving bowl and sprinkle the soaked cherries and the almonds on top. Grind pepper on top and serve with crackers or crusty bread.

ROASTED SQUASH WEDGES

Wedges of roasted squash strike a dramatic mood in this side dish. I leave the skin on for its texture and slight bitterness, which balances the sweetness of the squash flesh. The same recipe works with other varieties of winter squash, including butternut if that's easier to find. Richer-colored rosés, which can have a bit more body, match the texture of the squash, but there are a lot of other great wines to consider. Drinking a bone-dry, skin-contact wine with roasted squash is like drizzling bitter tahini sauce over it, offering savory contrast to the roasted sweetness. Lighter styles of Cabernet Franc or Cabernet Franc rosé, with their green pepper-ish flavors, can highlight the red pepper flakes. For less contrast and more of a match, a rich white wine also does the trick. The squash is delicious alongside Roasted Chicken Legs with Lemon, Radishes, and Capers (page 80).

SERVES 4 | DARKER-HUED ROSÉ AND CABERNET FRANC

---

1 medium acorn squash or 1 small kabocha squash (about 2 pounds), seeded and cut into 1- to 2-inch-thick wedges

1 tablespoon extra-virgin olive oil

½ teaspoon kosher salt

¼ teaspoon red pepper flakes

2 green onions, white and green parts, thinly sliced

¼ cup toasted pepitas or chopped toasted almonds

1 lemon wedge

Preheat the oven to 450°F.✦ Line a half-sheet pan with parchment paper or aluminum foil.

Put the squash wedges on the prepared pan and coat thoroughly with the oil. Season with the salt and red pepper flakes and arrange with a cut side down on the pan. Roast until the squash is tender and slightly charred, 25 to 30 minutes. Remove from the oven and immediately sprinkle the green onions and pepitas on top. Let them warm up and, in the case of the green onions, wilt a bit, about 5 minutes.

Transfer the squash to a platter, arranging the browned sides facing up. Squeeze the lemon wedge over the top and serve.

✦ If you have a convection setting on your oven, I highly encourage you to use it when roasting the squash because it will aid in caramelizing the edges. Set the oven at 425°F convection and monitor the final minutes for browning in case the squash is ready earlier.

POACHED SALMON WITH FENNEL-CELERY SALAD AND CAPER MAYO

Some people have a knack for putting together a meal in what looks to be a haphazard, last-minute way (cutting board askew, bits of herbs scattered across the counter). And still, it always comes out just so. Sandy Binder, an old family friend and terrific home cook, performs this magic trick every time she cooks salmon. I used to consider poaching salmon needlessly fussy—especially since salmon is perfectly delicious baked in the oven—but Sandy inspired me to plunge right in. The best part is it's a quick way to cook the fish simply, and you can use up yesterday's white wine in the poaching water. The result is fresh and light, and when served with sliced fennel and celery and a caper-spiked mayonnaise, it's a meal designed for warm nights when you don't want to heat up the kitchen much. Save the fennel fronds (the feathery stalks attached to the bulbs) for the poaching water and the mayo. If the fennel you buy doesn't come with fronds, it's okay to skip it.

For one of Sandy's salmon dinners, she poured us glasses of special-occasion Bandol rosé. Made from a blend of Mourvèdre, Grenache, and Cinsault—traditional Provençal grapes—it was so lively that it countered the salmon's rich, oily quality with refined acidity. The next rosé was deeper pink and had a bit less acidity. It didn't quite match the fish as well as the first, but we all still finished the bottle.

SERVES 4 | PROVENÇAL ROSÉ AND UNOAKED CHARDONNAY

1 pound skin-on salmon*

Kosher salt

3 tablespoons extra-virgin olive oil

6 cups water

1 bay leaf

1 fennel bulb, fronds separated and reserved (if available)

4 celery stalks

3 tablespoons fresh lemon juice

½ cup mayonnaise

2 tablespoons capers, drained and chopped

2 green onions, white and green parts, thinly sliced

1 cup white wine**

Freshly ground black pepper

Put the salmon on a plate 30 minutes to 1 hour before cooking. Sprinkle evenly with 1 teaspoon salt, then rub with 1 tablespoon of the oil, coating the pieces evenly. Let sit at room temperature while you prepare the poaching liquid.

In a wide pan 4 to 5 inches deep, combine the water, 2 teaspoons salt, and the bay leaf. Add 1 to 2 cups loosely packed fennel fronds (if you have them; reserve some fronds for the mayonnaise). Halve one of the celery stalks and add the pieces to the pan. Bring to a boil over high heat, then remove from the heat and let sit until you're ready to poach the salmon.

CONTINUED

POACHED SALMON WITH FENNEL-CELERY
SALAD AND CAPER MAYO, CONTINUED

Cut the fennel bulb in half lengthwise and cut out the core. Cut the bulb into thin slices lengthwise and put in a medium bowl. Thinly slice the remaining three celery stalks at an angle about the same thickness as the fennel and add them to the bowl with the fennel. Drizzle with the remaining 2 tablespoons oil and 2 tablespoons of the lemon juice. Sprinkle with a pinch of salt and toss to combine. Spoon onto a serving plate.

In a small bowl, mix together the mayonnaise, capers, green onions, and remaining 1 tablespoon lemon juice. Chop up about 2 tablespoons of the most feathery part of the fennel fronds and stir them into the mayonnaise.

Add the wine to the pan and bring the liquid to a boil over high heat. Add the salmon pieces one by one and turn the heat to medium-low. Poach the salmon until it is cooked through when pierced with the tip of a paring knife, 6 to 8 minutes. Very thick salmon pieces will still be medium-rare in the center; if you prefer it more cooked, cook for 1 to 2 minutes more.

Using a spatula or a large slotted spoon, gently lift out the salmon pieces and plate them with the celery and fennel. (Alternatively, you can transfer it to a separate plate and remove the skin before serving.) Grind pepper on top and serve with the caper mayo.

+ You can buy either four thinner portions (about 4 ounces each) or two thicker center-cut pieces (about 8 ounces each). If you buy one whole piece, cut it crosswise into four portions before starting.

++ An uncomplicated light and inexpensive white wine that you'd still want to drink is perfect for poaching fish. If you happen to have an open bottle in the refrigerator, even better.

ROASTED CHIPOTLE CHICKEN THIGHS

Growing up, we always had a jar of chipotle chiles en adobo in the back of the refrigerator, a holdover from my mom's childhood in Mexico City. Any time black beans or flank steak were on the table, out came the jar and my dad would habitually marvel at how chipotle made everything better. Here, the heat level is on the milder side, integrated with the other spices so it plays better with wine, though if you are a chile lover, add 2 tablespoons. For hot-weather refreshment, a cherry-red new-world rosé or deep-pink, serious Tavel rosé from France is a nice counterbalance to the chipotle. A deeper-hued orange wine also is exceptionally good and walks the line between heat, savory flavor, and orange zest. Or go in an entirely different direction and pick a bottle of red—Zinfandel from Lodi, California, has enough sweetness to tame the chipotles.

SERVES 4 | DEEP-RED ROSÉ AND ZINFANDEL

4 garlic cloves, minced

2 teaspoons kosher salt

1 tablespoon brown sugar (light or dark)

1 to 2 tablespoons chopped canned chipotle chiles en adobo, or 1 teaspoon ground chipotle chiles

1 tablespoon grated orange zest

2 teaspoons dried oregano

2 teaspoons sweet or smoked paprika

½ teaspoon ground cumin

¼ teaspoon ground cloves

2 tablespoons extra-virgin olive oil

8 bone-in, skin-on chicken thighs (5 to 7 ounces each)

2 green onions, white and green parts, thinly sliced

¼ cup coarsely chopped fresh cilantro

On a cutting board, sprinkle the garlic with the salt. Using the flat side of a knife, rub the salt into the garlic to create a paste. Put the paste in a large bowl and mix in the brown sugar, chipotle chiles, orange zest, oregano, paprika, cumin, and cloves. Stir in the oil.

Put the chicken in the bowl with the seasonings and rub each piece to coat. Cover and refrigerate for at least 4 hours or up to overnight. Remove the chicken from the refrigerator 1 hour before cooking.

Preheat the oven to 425°F. Line a half-sheet pan with parchment paper.

Put the chicken, skin-side up, on the prepared pan. Roast until the chicken skin is crisp and the juices run clear when the chicken is pierced with a knife, 35 to 40 minutes.

Serve the chicken sprinkled with the green onions and cilantro on top.

LAMB MEATBALLS WITH YOGURT SAUCE

Made with lamb and spiced with black pepper, oregano, and cumin, these Mediterranean-inspired meatballs have enough flavor that they're nearly just as good served at room temperature as they are hot. Finished with a tangy yogurt sauce and wrapped in flatbread, they're the perfect food for outdoor summer meals. Any extra yogurt sauce is great for drizzling over roasted squash (see page 99).

Try a couple of directions for wine: A new-world rosé with fresh strawberry–tart cherry notes is refreshing on warm evenings, while a full-bodied Syrah brings out the black pepper for cooler, cozier nights.

SERVES 4 | GRENACHE ROSÉ AND SYRAH

Meatballs

1 pound ground lamb

¼ cup water

3 garlic cloves, minced

2 green onions, white and green parts, thinly sliced, or ⅛ medium red onion, minced

1 teaspoon kosher salt

1 teaspoon paprika

1 teaspoon dried oregano

½ teaspoon ground cumin

¼ teaspoon freshly ground black pepper

½ cup panko bread crumbs✦

1 tablespoon extra-virgin olive oil

Yogurt Sauce

1 cup plain whole milk yogurt

1 cup firmly packed fresh cilantro leaves, chopped

2 tablespoons chopped fresh mint

1 garlic clove, grated with a Microplane or finely minced

¼ teaspoon kosher salt

Flatbread (such as lavash or pita) or buttery noodles for serving

✦ Panko bread crumbs are lighter in texture than classic dried bread crumbs, yielding meatballs that aren't as dense. If you have classic dried bread crumbs, use ⅓ cup. You can also use 1 cup fresh bread crumbs by blending day-old crusty bread in a food processor until it forms crumbs. For a gluten-free alternative, swap out the crumbs for ½ cup cooked rice and 1 lightly beaten egg to bind the meatballs together.

To make the meatballs: Preheat the oven to 450°F. Line a half-sheet pan with parchment paper or lightly oil it.

In a large bowl, gently but thoroughly mix together the lamb, water, garlic, green onions, salt, paprika, oregano, cumin, and pepper. Add the bread crumbs and gently mix until incorporated. Roll into 16 small meatballs about 1½ ounces each and arrange on the prepared pan. Brush the tops with the oil.

Roast, rotating the pan halfway through, until the tops of the meatballs start to brown, about 15 minutes. For a deeper brown color, carefully arrange an oven rack in the top third of the oven and preheat the broiler. Broil until the meatballs caramelize, 1 to 2 minutes depending on the broiler (keep a close eye on the pan and don't walk away while broiling).

To make the yogurt sauce: In a mini food processor, combine the yogurt, cilantro, mint, garlic, and salt and process until evenly blended. (Or chop the herbs very finely and stir the ingredients together in a bowl.)

Serve the meatballs with the yogurt sauce spooned over the top and flatbread on the side. For a more substantial plate, serve the meatballs and yogurt on top of buttery noodles.

PICNIC RED WINES

RED WINE GRAZING BOARD 110

PEPERONATA 113

GIARDINIERA 114

GREEN OLIVE TAPENADE 115

BROCCOLINI PASTA 116

EGGPLANT LAHMAJOON 118

The red-wine world is vast, ranging from light, juicy bottles all the way to the most brooding Barolo. But if Barolo (see Nebbiolo, page 124) is an age-for-years wine, the varieties in the picnic category are lighter, lower in tannins, and generally easygoing, whatever the food pairing. That's not to say these wines are never serious, but rather, they don't have to be. Serve picnic wines at room temperature or slightly chilled.

BARBERA

This grape has long been called the second-most important variety in Piedmont, the place in northern Italy that makes Barolo and Barbaresco out of the prized Nebbiolo grape. It's actually an unfair comparison because each has a role to play. While wines made of Nebbiolo need to age so their tannins soften, Barbera is ready to drink while relatively young. The two grapes complement each other—one for drinking now, one for drinking later. Barbera is one of Italy's most-planted red grapes, grown all over the country, and it can be made in a range of styles, from easygoing, low-alcohol, high-acid bottles to more complex versions. It's high in acidity but never lean, striking a balance between truly light reds (like red Alpine wines) and richer ones. It also grows outside of Italy in places settled by Italian immigrants, like California and Australia. At their best, Barbera wines are bright, crisp, and juicy, with notes of red cherries and wild berries, the perfect wine with pizza, braised chicken legs with polenta, or pasta with ragù. If you like Barbera, keep an eye out for Cesanese, a bright red wine made near Rome. And give Montepulciano a spin, too.

DOLCETTO

Grown around the same places as Barbera and Nebbiolo, Dolcetto is like the third child in an over-achieving family. It's fussier to grow than Barbera and sometimes takes itself too seriously, but its best mood is grapey and fresh. Its name means "little sweet one," though it's never sweet and can sometimes deliver a bit of bitterness thanks to its tannins. (The name comes from the grape's sweet flavor when eaten.) While some variations are made into bigger wines, Dolcetto is best when medium-bodied and fresh, with juicy grape and black cherry notes and vibrant aromas. If you like Dolcetto, dig deeper into grapes grown in the same neighborhoods, like Freisa, Grignolino, and Pelaverga.

GAMAY

Even if you've never sought out Gamay, chances are good you've heard of its most familiar wine: Beaujolais. Every year on the third Thursday of November, cases of Beaujolais Nouveau arrive at wine bars all over Paris, ushering in a night of bar crawling. Made by carbonic maceration, a method in which bunches of grapes sit in closed tanks filled with carbon dioxide, causing the fruit to ferment inside its skin, Beaujolais Nouveau is soft, juicy, and easy to drink. Yet this style isn't the only way to appreciate Gamay. In Oregon, the Loire Valley, and the Beaujolais region itself, winemakers also produce Gamay made like other reds (without the carbonic maceration), allowing for velvety, food-friendly wines. These versions of Gamay remain immediately drinkable but also are more complex and layered. Back in Beaujolais, the top wines come from ten specific villages and have become renown for their mineral elegance. To try them, look for "cru Beaujolais." The region has also become famous for being at the forefront of the natural wine movement (see page 14). With food, Gamay is perfect with charcuterie, cold cuts, hearty cheese, and pickles. Lighter styles can even be served a bit chilled on hot days. If you like Gamay, try País from Chile.

MONTEPULCIANO

This red grape often gets described as "juicy in a deep purple, big shoulders kind of way." And while there's nothing wrong with that description, it's not the whole story. While the grape is one of Italy's most-planted varieties, its origins lie in the foothills of the Apennines in Abruzzo, where (before global warming) it was hard to get grapes to ripen. The ripening problem led to a style of wine called Cerasuolo ("cherry"), which still exists today. Think of Cerasuolo as either a rosé with depth and tannins or a light red wine—no matter what, it's an amazing food wine, able to pair with everything from grilled meat to delicate fish and vegetables. Cerasuolo aside, Montepulciano is also made into rounder, more fruit-forward wines for drinking now (though there are exceptions). The best examples are fresh and medium bodied, imbued with red or purple fruits and Mediterranean herbs. Montepulciano shines with red-sauce pasta and pizza. It's fair to say that I'm a big fan, and I think this wine just doesn't get the kind of praise it deserves! If you like Montepulciano and want to lean into more Italian reds, try Chianti Classico, which is made with Sangiovese (see page 125). Also consider exploring other juicy Italian wines, like Piedirosso, Frappato, and Ciliegiolo.

VALPOLICELLA

In the 1990s, when everyone seemed to be chasing the biggest, richest red wines they could find, Valpolicella was nearly forgotten next to its cousin, Amarone, a wine with the same blend of grapes but made in a style that was much more concentrated and weighty. While Amarone is best sipped after dinner, red cherry–imbued Valpolicella will be at your side all the way through the meal. The big difference is Valpolicella grapes are crushed fresh, while grapes for Amarone are left to raisin for a few weeks or months, making the resulting wine nearly sweet. But since leaner, brighter wines are much easier to pair with food, Valpolicella is coming into its own these days. The wine is a blend of local grapes from Italy's Veneto region, mainly Corvina and a motley crew of other varieties. There's also a style called ripasso, in which fermented Valpolicella wine is poured over the spent skins from Amarone making, but I favor the fresher versions with cured meats, cheeses, and even shellfish. If you like Valpolicella, seek out Vernatsch (see opposite page). Also seek out Chiaretto, a style of rosé wine made with similar grapes as Valpolicella.

ALPINE RED WINES

Right after college, a friend and I did the hopping-around-Europe-on-a-budget thing. Through either friends or family connections or sheer will, we found ourselves in Switzerland drinking the local red from bottles capped with beer tops. The wine may have been Merlot, but it was bright and simple, and this may have been the first time I was exposed to Alpine-style wines. Nowadays, these lighter, brighter reds with delicate flavors are much more popular. With mouth-watering acidity, they can stand up to everything from gochujang-spiked bibimbap to black bean quesadillas. Look for the following mountain-style reds:

Trousseau from the Jura, a region in France bordering the Alps (and now also grown in Northern California)

Red wines from the Savoie, a mountain region in France bordering Italy and Switzerland (grapes include Gamay, Mondeuse, and Persan)

Red wines from Valle d'Aosta, a region in Italy bordering France and Switzerland near Mont Blanc (grapes include Cornalin, Fumin, Petit Rouge, and Picotener, the local strain of Nebbiolo)

Vernatsch (also called Trollinger in German and Schiava in Italian) from Alto Adige, a region in Italy in the foothills of the Dolomites bordering Austria

RED WINE GRAZING BOARD

Like the White Wine Cheese Board (page 74), the idea here is to create a bountiful table that doesn't involve any last-minute cooking. The best versions combine a few homemade garnishes and condiments made in advance, like quick pickles and simple tapenades, with pâté or prosciutto or any other specialty meats from a good deli counter. Light, lower-alcohol red wines, like Oregon Gamay, are a great place to start, while Barbera and Dolcetto will provide a bit more acidity. My suggestion? Try them all and keep your friends well fed so they'll stay awhile.

SERVES 6 TO 8-ISH | GAMAY, BARBERA, AND DOLCETTO

1 wedge hard cheese (such as aged pecorino, Parmigiano-Reggiano, or dry Jack), broken into chunks

2 or 3 types of meat (such as prosciutto, soppressata, salumi, or pâté), or add another cheese

Green Olive Tapenade (page 115)

Peperonata (page 113) or Giardiniera (page 114)

Onion Jam (page 142)

Cornichons, olives, or assorted pickles

1 baguette, sliced, and/or crackers (Savory Cheddar Shortbread, page 140, or Sea Salt Crackers, page 56)

There's no need for specifics; just ensure that the cheese is at room temperature and the meat isn't ice cold. Assemble the tapenade, peperonata, jam, cornichons, and baguette so it's simple for everyone to help themselves and load up their plate. Offer toothpicks or forks to make it easy for people to come back for seconds or to spear a cornichon now and again.

Peperonata

When grapes grow with too many leaves shading the vines, the resulting wines can exhibit a green bell pepper flavor. For years I filed away "green pepper" as an undesirable taste in wine, but I've grown to love how a green pepper accent can season fruit flavor with a touch of vegetal austerity. Cabernet Franc is known for making wines that often have distinctive green pepper notes, and light, juicy styles of Sangiovese can also carry an herbal edge accented with red cherries. Not that you have to drink a wine with green pepper flavors when eating roasted peppers (Montepulciano isn't known for it and it's great here). Peperonata makes for a satisfying option on a grazing board or as a side dish with grilled sausages, and a red wine with an herbaceous underbelly would hit the right notes all around.

| MAKES ABOUT 2 CUPS | CABERNET FRANC, SANGIOVESE, AND MONTEPULCIANO |

---

4 bell peppers, preferably a mix of colors

2 tablespoons extra-virgin olive oil

2 tablespoons capers, drained and patted dry

¼ medium red onion, thinly sliced

Kosher salt

¼ teaspoon red pepper flakes

1 tablespoon white or red wine vinegar

Preheat the oven to 450°F.

Put the bell peppers on a half-sheet pan and evenly coat with 1 tablespoon of the oil. Roast, turning the peppers over once or twice, until the skins pull away from the flesh, 20 to 25 minutes. (Alternatively, grill the peppers over a medium-hot grill until blistered.) Transfer the peppers to a large bowl and put a plate on top or cover with plastic wrap to let them steam, which loosens their skins.

When the peppers are cool enough to handle but still warm, peel away the skins with your hands. Halve the peppers lengthwise, discard the seeds and core, and cut into thick strips.

In a large sauté pan over medium heat, warm the remaining 1 tablespoon oil. Add the capers and fry until they open up like tiny flowers and become crispy, about 1 minute. Add the onion, ¼ teaspoon salt, and the red pepper flakes and cook, stirring occasionally, until the onion has softened, 2 to 3 minutes, lowering the heat if the onion starts to scorch.

Add the roasted peppers and vinegar and cook, stirring occasionally, until the pan is dry, about 1 minute. Taste, adding more salt if desired. Serve the peppers warm or at room temperature. The peppers can be stored in an airtight container in the refrigerator for up to 1 week.

Giardiniera

There are two schools of thought about giardiniera: some say it's a pickled pepper condiment, others say it's merely pickles. No judgment—both are good—and the debate is largely geographical. If you live in Chicago, chances are you're in the former camp. If you live elsewhere, you're in the latter. This recipe is inspired by Midwestern chef Paul Virant's version, and it's more of a pickle than a condiment. Paul salts the vegetables to leach out water, then rinses off the extra salt, which makes the vegetables tender and primed to soak up brine. To serve as part of a spread with salumi and cheese, spoon the pickled vegetables into a bowl and drizzle good olive oil on top. Giardiniera alone isn't a seamless match with wine, but when enjoyed with cheese and meat, it's perfect with low-tannin, juicy reds, like Gamay from Oregon and Frappato from Sicily.

MAKES ABOUT 1 QUART | GAMAY AND FRAPPATO

½ small head cauliflower, cut into florets, larger pieces halved (about 2 cups)

½ fennel bulb, cored and thinly sliced lengthwise, or 2 celery stalks, cut crosswise into ½-inch pieces

1 medium carrot, peeled and cut crosswise at a slight angle into 1-inch pieces

⅛ medium red onion, thinly sliced

¼ cup kosher salt

1¼ cups water

1 cup white or red wine vinegar

1 tablespoon granulated sugar

1 garlic clove, halved lengthwise

¼ teaspoon red pepper flakes

Extra-virgin olive oil for drizzling

Have a heatproof 1-quart jar and lid ready.

In a large bowl, mix together the cauliflower, fennel, carrot, onion, and salt, using your hands to ensure all the pieces are coated. Put the vegetables in a colander set in a large bowl to catch the water and set aside to drain for 1 hour.

After 1 hour, a small pool of water should be in the base of the bowl and the vegetables will look a bit wilted, as if they've been briefly cooked. Rinse the vegetables thoroughly with cold water and drain well for a few minutes. Put the vegetables in the jar.

In a small saucepan, combine the 1¼ cups water, vinegar, sugar, garlic, and red pepper flakes and bring to a boil over high heat to dissolve the sugar, 2 to 3 minutes. While the brine is still hot, pour it over the vegetables. If some of the vegetables are not covered in the brine, heat up a bit of water and pour it over the top—there is enough vinegar in the brine that it can stand a bit more water without losing its punch.

Let sit, uncovered, at room temperature until cool, then screw on the lid. The giardiniera is best when made about 2 days ahead of serving. It keeps in the refrigerator for 4 months. When ready to serve, scoop the vegetables out of the jar and drizzle oil over the top until the pickles are shiny.

Green Olive Tapenade

Green olive tapenade is a sneaky-easy condiment that tastes a little brighter than classic black olive tapenade. It's perfect for eating with mild cheeses, spooning over roasted asparagus and braised artichokes, or spreading on crusty bread. Expect this tapenade to be salty, though exactly how salty depends on the green olives themselves: if you prefer less salt, soak the capers in water for 5 minutes, then rinse well. While tapenade alone doesn't constitute a pairing with wine, it's a great condiment to have on hand for a picnic of cured meats, cheeses, and vegetables paired with light, juicy red wines. It's also great alongside crisp white wines (see pages 51 to 53).

In a mini food processor, combine the olives, capers, anchovies (if using), parsley, garlic, red pepper flakes, and lemon zest. (A standard-size food processor also works, but be prepared to scrape down the sides of the processor more frequently, with the machine turned off each time.) Pulse until the mixture barely comes together. Add the oil and pulse to incorporate, then taste, adding more oil for a milder tapenade. (Alternatively, finely chop the olives, capers, anchovies, parsley, and garlic and then mix together in a medium bowl with the red pepper flakes, lemon zest, and oil.)

The tapenade can be stored in an airtight container in the refrigerator for up to 2 weeks, but is best a day or two after making. Let it come to room temperature before serving.

MAKES ABOUT 1 CUP | GRENACHE AND CÔTES DU RHÔNE

---

1 cup pitted green olives (such as Castelvetrano or a mix)✦

2 teaspoons capers, drained

4 oil-packed anchovy fillets, or 1 teaspoon anchovy paste (optional)✦✦

½ cup loosely packed fresh flat-leaf parsley leaves

1 garlic clove, minced

¼ teaspoon red pepper flakes

Grated zest of 1 lemon

⅓ cup extra-virgin olive oil, plus more as needed

✦ See page 28 for pitting instructions.

✦✦ See page 28 about anchovies.

BROCCOLINI PASTA

I learned to cook in restaurants when "big pot blanching"—the fine-dining method of boiling green vegetables in an enormous pot of boiling salted water—was the final word in green vegetable cookery. The vegetables retained their green color, boiling just long enough to soften before being plunged into icy water. The technique nearly ruined me for appreciating cooking vegetables in a crowded pot until they turned army green, but that is what's required to make this pasta. When I was very much still in my big-pot blanching phase, I visited Puglia in southern Italy and saw a pot crowded with leafy broccoli rabe and orecchiette pasta cooking together. The results looked plain, but the deep flavors have pushed me to replicate this pasta ever since. Puglia is the land of easygoing red and rosato (rosé) wines made with grapes such as Negroamaro and Primitivo. Those reds, as well as a lighter-style Montepulciano or deep-pink rosé, are all excellent partners with this pasta.

SERVES 4 | PRIMITIVO, MONTEPULCIANO, AND NEGROAMARO

12 ounces broccolini (about 2 small bunches)+

¼ cup extra-virgin olive oil

5 garlic cloves, thinly sliced

½ teaspoon red pepper flakes, plus more as needed

Kosher salt

12 ounces dried short-style pasta (such as rigatoni, penne, or orecchiette)

1 ounce grated Parmesan or pecorino cheese (1 cup if finely grated with a Microplane; ½ cup if grated with a box grater)

1 lemon (optional)

+ You can substitute leafy broccoli rabe or broccoli florets for the broccolini. Go by the weight measurement; essentially you want equal portions pasta to vegetable. For broccoli rabe, use everything, from the leaves and small florets to the stems, and cut everything into roughly the same-size pieces. For broccoli florets, halve or quarter the larger florets. If the stems are thick, slice them into thin coins.

Trim the ends and cut the broccolini crosswise so the stems and heads are about the same size.

In a small saucepan over medium-low heat, combine the oil and garlic and gently bring to a simmer. Cook until the garlic turns a very light shade of brown, about 30 seconds. Pour the contents of the pan into a small heatproof bowl and stir in the red pepper flakes and ½ teaspoon salt.

Bring a large pot of salted water to a boil over high heat. Add the pasta and cook for 6 minutes. Stir in the broccolini and cook until the pasta is cooked through but not too soft and the broccolini is tender, 4 to 5 minutes. Scoop out ½ cup of the pasta cooking water, then drain the pasta and broccolini.

Return the pasta and broccolini to the pot and stir in the garlic oil and half of the reserved pasta cooking water. Bring to a simmer over medium heat and cook, stirring to break up the pieces of broccolini. Mix in half of the cheese. If using the lemon, zest it directly into the pot. If the pasta looks a bit dry, mix in 1 tablespoon or more of the reserved cooking water.

Transfer the pasta to a warmed serving bowl and garnish with the remaining cheese. Season with more salt or red pepper flakes if desired.

EGGPLANT LAHMAJOON

Lahmajoon is often called Armenian pizza, though it's not really a true pizza. For one, there's no cheese. There's no sauce either—the topping is a mix of ground lamb or beef with spices, herbs, and a bit of tomato and red pepper paste. Still, with the birthplace of bread being somewhere around Jordan and Iran, this staple Middle Eastern flatbread may have been a precursor to Neapolitan pizza. In Armenian bakeries around Glendale and Fresno, California, and in LA's Little Armenia, you can buy these in stacks to reheat at home. This recipe is the meatless eggplant version, which is great for summertime eating. If it's too hot to crank up the oven, make the topping and serve it as a dip with crackers.

The combination of eggplant and tomatoes calls for wines with high acidity and low tannins, like Barbera, or juicy, red wines, like Malbec and Grenache. If you want to get into the true spirit of lahmajoon, pour a red Armenian wine made with the Areni grape.

| MAKES 4 LAHMAJOON | BARBERA, GRENACHE, GRENACHE ROSÉ, AND MALBEC |

Dough

4 cups (560 g) all-purpose flour, plus more for dusting

1½ cups (360 ml) room-temperature water

1¼ teaspoons kosher salt

Topping

4 tablespoons extra-virgin olive oil

1 eggplant (a smallish Italian or globe variety; about 1 pound), cut into ½-inch cubes

1½ teaspoons kosher salt

One 14.5-ounce can diced tomatoes with juices

1 tablespoon tomato paste

½ small red onion, coarsely chopped (about ¾ cup)

1 cup loosely packed fresh flat-leaf parsley leaves or a mix of parsley, mint, cilantro, and/or dill

2 garlic cloves, thinly sliced

1 teaspoon paprika

½ teaspoon ground cumin

½ teaspoon dried oregano

¼ teaspoon red pepper flakes

Extra-virgin olive oil for drizzling

½ cup plain whole milk yogurt

Chopped fresh herbs (such as mint and dill), and pickled red onions or pepperoncini, thinly sliced, for serving (optional)

Lemon wedges for serving

To make the dough: In a large bowl, mix the flour, water, and salt together with your hands until a shaggy dough forms. Dust a work surface lightly with flour, then turn the dough out onto the surface and knead until it starts to come together, about 3 minutes. (Knead by pressing the heel of your hand into the dough and pushing the dough away from you, then dragging it back with your hand and repeating.) Return the dough to the bowl, cover with a kitchen towel, and let rest while you make the topping. (If you prefer to prepare the topping ahead, make the dough and let it rest for 20 minutes before cutting and rolling it out.)

To make the topping: In a large sauté pan over medium-high heat, warm 2 tablespoons of the oil. Add half of the eggplant, season with ¾ teaspoon of the salt, and cook, stirring often, until the eggplant is soft in the center and has reduced in size by nearly half, about 6 minutes. Transfer to a food processor. Repeat to cook the remaining eggplant using the same amount of oil and salt, then transfer to the processor.

CONTINUED

EGGPLANT LAHMAJOON, CONTINUED

Add the tomatoes and juices, tomato paste, onion, parsley, garlic, paprika, cumin, oregano, and red pepper flakes to the processor and blend until a chunky puree forms. (You should have about 4 cups.) Let cool to room temperature. If not using right away, cover and refrigerate. You can spread the topping on the flatbread while it is still chilled.

Preheat the oven to 500°F.✦ Have two half-sheet pans ready as well as four sheets of parchment paper cut to fit the pans. (The lahmajoon will be baked one at a time, and the parchment makes it easier to transfer the dough to the pans and free up the pans for the next batch.)

Dust a work surface lightly with flour and put the dough on top. Cut into four pieces and roll each piece into a ball. Dust a rolling pin with flour and roll out one piece of dough into a wide oval long enough to fill the parchment paper (at least 13 inches long). It's better for the dough to be too thin than too thick. Carefully transfer the first oval to the parchment paper and place on one of the sheet pans. Bake until slightly puffed and golden brown in a few spots, about 5 minutes. While the first pan bakes, roll out the next round of dough, then bake it like the first. If the dough is stubborn and resists being rolled out, let the piece rest some more and start on another piece. Repeat the rolling and baking process until you have a stack of four baked ovals. Keep the oven at 500°F.

When the baked dough is cool enough to handle, spread just under 1 cup of the topping over each piece in an even layer, smoothing it to the edges and ensuring it's not too thick in places. Bake one lahmajoon at a time until the edges are crisp and browned in spots, 7 to 10 minutes.

Top with a drizzle of oil, a spoonful of yogurt, and herbs and pickled onions (if desired). Serve with lemon wedges. Leftovers can be stored in an airtight container in the refrigerator for up to 5 days and reheated in a toaster oven. Once topped and baked, lahmajoon also can be frozen for up to 1 month. Bake from frozen at 400°F until heated all the way through and crisp on the edges.

✦ If you have a baking stone or a baking steel, preheat the oven with the stone or steel on the center rack. The stone or steel will help the bottom of the lahmajoon bake faster, giving it a slight char.

REASONABLY SERIOUS RED WINES

GARLICKY MARINATED MUSHROOMS 126

CARAMELIZED CABBAGE
AND ONION GALETTE 128

BEET AND POTATO SALAD
WITH TARRAGON 131

ROASTED RADICCHIO WITH BEANS 133

ORANGE AND FENNEL PORK LOIN ROAST 134

Take "serious" with a big caveat: some of these wines can be serious, but in the hands of a different producer or when made in a different area, they can be more reminiscent of juicy picnic wine. Still, since some are collector wines, they can be as serious as it gets. At the very least, they're the wines you want to think about for a few beats after a first sip and before the second. Serve at a cool room temperature.

CABERNET FRANC

In a way, Cabernet Franc is the red-grape version of white grape Chenin Blanc (see page 65), which was also a once-forgotten, now-beloved grape from the Loire Valley. Even though Cabernet Franc is used as a blending grape in Bordeaux, it comes into its own around the Loire towns of Chinon and Bourgueil, where the wines can be an amazing combination of red fruit and green pepper. Some Cabernet Franc from this area can be more substantial, but other bottles are light and can even be served chilled. You can also look for these wines from New York State's Finger Lakes region, where the red wine has come into its own; the cooler climate keeps the wines tart and high in acidity, perfect for rich sausages or stuffed peppers. Cabernet Franc made into rosé can be a revelation, slightly deeper and more serious than standard-issue rosé but no less enjoyable. If you like Cabernet Franc, you may like the herbaceousness found in Sangiovese.

GARNACHA/GRENACHE

While this is still under dispute, Spain's granite soils may be the origin of Garnacha, a variety that also thrives in Sardinia (under the name Cannonau) and in the south of France (as Grenache). At its best, Garnacha is more about acidity than tannins and structure. When grown at higher altitudes, the wines are fresh and fruity, with notes of strawberries or blackberries, while also carrying herbs and sometimes spice. The grape is key in Priorat, a small region in Catalonia known for full-bodied reds, but not all Garnacha/Grenache wines are quite as big. Some can actually be quite juicy and perfect for picnics. Aged sheep's cheeses, like Manchego, and Spain's famous jamón are easy matches with Spanish Garnacha, but it also holds up to cumin lamb stir-fry and sauces with chiles. If you like Garnacha/Grenache, explore the whole international family. In France, jammy Châteauneuf-du-Pape and lighter, every day Côtes du Rhône wines frequently use Grenache as the main grape in their blends. In Sardinia, Cannonau deliver flavors of red fruits and Mediterranean herbs as the island's signature red. Grenache (and white grape Grenache Blanc) are also grown in California, Oregon, and Australia.

NEBBIOLO

Allegedly named for the fog (nebbia) that rolls into Piedmont in Northern Italy, Nebbiolo has staked its claim as one of Italy's most-treasured native grapes, creating wines that evoke rose petal, leather, and even tar—all in a good way. The grape is also famous for the way it expresses the area around it, much like Pinot Noir. The most famous Nebbiolo wines are Barolo and Barbaresco, and within those areas are specific vineyards that carry a specific name, a sign of how seriously everyone takes these wines. For years, though, Nebbiolo's high levels of acidity and tannins made the wines something you couldn't think of opening until bottles had achieved a fine patina of dust in someone's cellar. In the late twentieth century, however, there was a revolution of sorts and some younger winemakers in the Barolo and Barbaresco winegrowing areas started to change techniques, making wines that were easier to drink at a younger age. You wouldn't believe the controversy this stirred up! Since then, most winemakers have moved on from the fights between the so-called traditionalists and modernists and returned to focus on producing great wine. Not all Nebbiolo wines come from Barolo and Barbaresco. A half-day's drive from there will take you to Alto Piemonte, where Nebbiolo wines from the areas around the towns of Gattinara, Boca, and the like tend to be lighter and brighter and definitely worth seeking out. The regions of Lombardy and Valle d'Aosta make lighter and mountain-style versions at high altitudes. Some believe Valtellina, a historic region in the far north of Lombardy near Switzerland, is the birthplace of Nebbiolo. Also look for Langhe Nebbiolo, which is made all around the general area of Barolo and Barbaresco but is often ready to drink at an earlier age. Egg yolk–rich pasta dishes, braised beef, and anything with mushrooms are all classic pairings with Nebbiolo wines. If you like Nebbiolo, seek out Etna Rosso made from a blend of grapes grown on Sicily's active volcano.

PINOT NOIR

Pinot Noir is tricky to understand: It is an ancient grape that makes some of the world's most expensive wines that come from tiny subplots within vineyard land so famous that wine connoisseurs memorize the direction its hillsides face (before climate change, a southern exposure meant more sun and better ripening conditions). But it's also so popular that nearly every country that makes wine also makes Pinot Noir. What makes it so beloved is how it can express the area in which it's grown. The grape makes wines that are light and subtle as well as complex, capable of aging for years but also ready to drink when young. Because Pinot Noir delivers high acidity, it's an amazing food wine. Burgundy has set the benchmark for Pinot Noir, but few people can afford the best bottles anymore and there are also stunning versions from elsewhere, such as southern Germany, northern Italy, coastal California, Oregon's Willamette Valley, and New Zealand. Expect red-fruit flavors, like cranberry and raspberry, wrapped up with dried herb or mushroom earthiness. The best wines are restrained but immediately enjoyable. For food, think mushrooms, roasted cabbage, braised chicken, and a range of cheeses, from aged goat and Brie to funky washed-rind Taleggio.

Because Pinot Noir is not as high in tannins as grapes such as Cabernet Sauvignon and Syrah, it also works well with richly spiced dishes, including coconut-based curries and tandoori chicken. For these foods, pick out a bottle from countries outside of Europe. If you like Pinot Noir but want a fruit-filled alternative, try Gamay.

RIOJA/TEMPRANILLO

Spain is like a new wine frontier with a very old wine history. A brutal civil war in the 1930s followed by decades of living under a dictatorship took the country on a very long detour through tough times before it could reacquaint itself with its centuries-old wine-making heritage. We will likely be hearing a lot more about the breadth of Spanish wines in the years to come. Today, though, it's hard to talk about Spain without discussing Rioja, a layered and often age-worthy wine made with mostly Tempranillo, Spain's most important red grape, along with Garnacha and a few other native grapes grown at more than 1,500 feet above sea level and blended together.

The precise style of Rioja varies from more restrained, earthy blends filled with tobacco and leather to more extroverted renditions evocative of Napa Valley reds. Rioja also offers some of the best wine values on the market, especially if you want to taste aged red wines without having to age them yourself; look for bottlings labeled "reserva" (aged three years before release) or "gran reserva" (aged five years before release). Crianza wines are the youngest, aging for two years before release. If you like Rioja, seek out Sangiovese or Nebbiolo.

SANGIOVESE

One of Italy's most important red grapes, Sangiovese yields wines that can be light and juicy or linear and serious, but most of the time, it's something in between: a tart, medium-bodied wine with a bit of grip to it. At its best, it's a beautiful mix of red cherries, cranberries, and fennel grounded in earthiness, and it always has a lot of acidity. The grape itself is a fussy variety, not easy to grow or harvest, but it thrives in places with warm days, cool nights, and long, sunny summers (which, to me, sounds less about being fussy and more about living your best Mediterranean life). Sangiovese is the grape behind these well-known wines: Chianti Classico, Vino Nobile di Montepulciano, and Brunello di Montalcino. Some of which are built to age and can be a bit serious. A good place to get started is with lighter, less expensive Rosso di Montepulciano and Rosso di Montalcino, also made with Sangiovese. (Rosso di Montepulciano has no relation to the Montepulciano grape; see page 108.) Outside of Tuscany, some of the best Sangiovese-based wines are Sangiovese di Romagna and Montefalco Rosso.

With food, you can't go wrong with salty salumi, prosciutto, or marinated mushrooms. Sangiovese is also perfect with eggplant, tomatoes, and tomato-based sauces, and is a classic match with rich pork braises and sausages. If you like Sangiovese but want a wine that's a little more off the beaten path, try Teroldego or Lagrein, two reds from northern Italy.

GARLICKY MARINATED MUSHROOMS

I used to be in the camp of cooking mushrooms over high heat to get them to brown while evaporating off their water, but Andrea Nguyen's book *Vietnamese Food Any Day* gave me an alternate approach inspired by Vietnamese clay pot cooking. I love the technique for its simplicity: Put mushrooms in a heavy pot (I use my small 2-quart Dutch oven), drizzle the oil over the top, cover, and *then* turn on the heat. The mushrooms gradually release their liquid as they warm up and sort of marinate in their own juices as they cook. It's the best and most hands-off way to create a side dish for earthy red wine such as Nebbiolo from Alto Piemonte—the northern part of Italy's Piedmont region—or a mellow, traditional Rioja. Finish off the spread with some cheese, bread, and salumi.

MAKES ABOUT 1 CUP | NEBBIOLO AND RIOJA

---

12 ounces cremini or button mushrooms

2 tablespoons extra-virgin olive oil

¼ teaspoon kosher salt

Freshly ground black pepper

2 garlic cloves, smashed

3 sprigs thyme or oregano, or ½ teaspoon dried thyme or oregano

2 teaspoons balsamic vinegar

Flaky sea salt

Wash the mushrooms well, then trim off the stem ends (leave the stems in place unless they look a bit withered). If any of the mushrooms are much larger than others, halve them through the stem end.

In a medium heavy-bottomed saucepan or small Dutch oven, add the mushrooms. Drizzle the oil over the top, then cover, set over medium heat, and cook without stirring until you hear sizzling, 2 to 3 minutes. Uncover, season with the kosher salt and a few grinds of pepper, and give the mushrooms a stir. Put the garlic and thyme on top, then cover, turn the heat to low, and let the mushrooms gently steam without stirring for 12 minutes.

Uncover and check the texture of the mushrooms. If they are still firm and there isn't much liquid in the pot, cover and continue to cook for 3 minutes more, then check again. If the mushrooms are soft, leave them uncovered, increase the heat, and simmer until most of the water has evaporated, 1 or 2 minutes. Remove from the heat and stir in the vinegar. Transfer the mushrooms to a bowl and let cool to room temperature. Store in an airtight container in the refrigerator for up to 1 week. Serve at room temperature topped with pinches of flaky sea salt and more pepper, if desired.

CARAMELIZED CABBAGE AND ONION GALETTE

The handmade look of a galette prepared with a buttery piecrust pastry is inviting and casual, signaling that it's perfectly okay to cut right into it, leaving a trail of crumbs behind. This savory fall- and winter-ready galette gives everyday ingredients, like cabbage and onions, a chance to shine. The key to the deepest flavor comes from allowing the topping to cook down and brown a bit before baking the galette. Serve a mild to medium Alpine-style cheese, like Gruyère, alongside. Avoid strong cheeses, such as blue cheese, which can overpower the galette as well as wines such as Pinot Noir. For bottles, if you want to extend beyond Pinot, look for red wines from cool, alpine areas (see page 109). The galette also pairs well with whites that fall on the richer side, like unoaked appley Chardonnay. You can make both the dough and the topping a couple of days ahead, then assemble and bake the galette the day you plan to serve it. If you have any oven-dried grapes (see page 77) on hand, add them to the topping right before baking for an extra bit of sweetness.

SERVES 6 | PINOT NOIR AND ALPINE RED WINES

Pastry Dough

1 cup plus 2 tablespoons (155 g) all-purpose flour, plus more for dusting

¼ teaspoon kosher salt

8 tablespoons (1 stick) (113 g) cold unsalted butter, cut into small cubes

3 tablespoons ice water

1 tablespoon apple cider vinegar

Topping

1 tablespoon extra-virgin olive oil

½ yellow onion, thinly sliced

1 cup thinly sliced green cabbage (about ⅛ head)

1 medium green or Fuji apple, grated

1 teaspoon chopped fresh thyme

¼ teaspoon kosher salt

⅛ teaspoon freshly ground black pepper

Gruyère or tomme/toma cheese for serving

To make the pastry dough: Put the flour in a large bowl and whisk in the salt. Gently rub the butter into the flour using your thumbs and fingertips, running your hands over different areas until all of the butter cubes have been rubbed into the flour and there are no butter pieces larger than a dried bean.

In a glass measuring cup, mix the water and vinegar together and pour into the flour mixture. Gently mix the flour and water together with your hands until a shaggy dough forms, then knead gently by pressing the heel of your hand into the dough so it compacts against the base of the bowl and comes together. Transfer to a lightly dusted work surface, pat into a 6-inch disk, and place in an airtight container (or wrap in plastic wrap) and refrigerate for at least 1 hour or up to 5 days.

To make the topping: In a large skillet over medium-high heat, warm the oil. Add the onion, turn the heat to medium, and cook, stirring occasionally, until softened and golden, 3 to 5 minutes, lowering the heat as needed to prevent scorching. Add the cabbage, increase the heat to medium-high, and cook, stirring occasionally, until wilted and slightly brown, about 4 minutes. Stir in the apple, thyme, salt, and pepper and simmer briefly until any apple juices have evaporated. Transfer the contents of the pan to a medium bowl and let cool to room temperature. (You will have about 1 cup.) The topping can be stored in an airtight container in the refrigerator for up to 5 days.

Position a rack in the upper third of the oven and preheat to 400°F. Line a half-sheet pan with parchment paper.

Let the dough sit at room temperature until soft enough to roll out but still cold, about 10 minutes. Dust a work surface and rolling pin lightly with flour, put the dough on top of the surface, and flatten into a thinner disk. Roll out the dough into a 14-inch round or an oval roughly the same size and transfer to the prepared sheet pan. If you have time and the space in the refrigerator, chill the dough for 15 minutes.

Pile the topping in the center of the dough in an even layer, leaving a 2-inch border. Fold the uncovered edges inward by about 1½ inches, pleating the dough to form a crust and gently pressing to adhere. Brush the crust with water.

Bake the galette, rotating the pan after 15 minutes, until the crust is golden brown and the filling is lightly caramelized, 35 to 38 minutes. Let cool to room temperature before cutting into wedges. Serve the galette with cheese alongside.

BEET AND POTATO SALAD WITH TARRAGON

Countries in the former Soviet Union all seem to serve salat vinaigrette—a beet, bean, and potato salad seasoned with dill pickles. There actually isn't any vinaigrette in it, just the pickles for acidity. The versions I've tried are usually seasoned with dill or a combination of dill and parsley, and it's delightful. Here, I take the salad in a slightly different direction, playing up the iron-rich, sweet flavors of red beets with tarragon. It's an earthy, fragrant side for roast chicken or pork loin or can be part of a spread with salty cheeses, like feta. Something about cherry-flavored Valpolicella, the lighter-weight cousin of Amarone, seems to work with the beets, but other fruit-forward reds with a little earthy accent, like Garnacha/Grenache, play well, too. A deeper-hued, rich orange wine also pairs with this beautifully.

SERVES 4 TO 6 | VALPOLICELLA, GARNACHA/GRENACHE, AND ORANGE WINE

---

4 red baby beets (or the smallest beets you can find), trimmed of greens and stringy root tips (about 8 ounces)

Kosher salt

1 pound Yukon gold potatoes, cut into 1-inch pieces

2 tablespoons extra-virgin olive oil

½ medium red onion, sliced

2 large or 3 small dill pickles, cut into ½-inch pieces

2 tablespoons dill pickle brine, or 1 tablespoon white wine vinegar

1 tablespoon chopped fresh tarragon✦

✦ If you don't have tarragon, chopped dill, basil, or chervil are all good substitutions.

Put the beets in a medium pot, add enough water to cover, and season with a big pinch of salt. Bring to a boil over high heat, lower the heat, and simmer gently until the beets are tender when pierced with the tip of a knife, 20 to 25 minutes for small beets and 40 to 45 minutes for larger ones. Drain. When the beets are cool enough to handle, use your fingers or a paring knife to remove the skins (do this while the beets are still warm or the skins will stick). Cut the beets into ½-inch wedges.

Rinse the pot, fill it with water, and add a big pinch of salt. Bring to a boil over high heat. Add the potatoes and return the water to a boil. Lower the heat and simmer gently until the potatoes are tender when pierced with the tip of a knife, about 15 minutes. Drain and let cool to room temperature, about 15 minutes. Transfer the potatoes to a large bowl.

In a large skillet over medium heat, warm the oil. Add the onion and cook, stirring often, until softened, 3 to 4 minutes. Stir in the beets, pickles, and pickle brine and season with ¼ teaspoon salt. Pour the contents of the pan into the bowl with the potatoes. Add the tarragon and mix to combine. Taste, seasoning with ¼ teaspoon salt or less (some pickles and pickle brines are saltier than others, so you may not need any more). Serve at room temperature. The salad can be stored in an airtight container in the refrigerator for up to 4 days; taste and reseason if needed.

ROASTED RADICCHIO WITH BEANS

This is a pretty side dish that doubles as a light meal if an at-home happy hour stretches into dinner. Beans are magic with nearly any style of wine, but this dish gets a red-wine edge with radicchio. Roasting radicchio in a hot oven tames its bitterness, making it friendlier to eat alongside a range of wines, especially those that taste bright and juicy, like Barbera. Or go a bit earthier and add toasted hazelnuts on top to serve with Pinot Noir from Oregon. Because of the creamy beans and complexity of the roasted radicchio, richer-style white wines with acidity, like Verdicchio from Italy, are also good matches.

SERVES 4 | PINOT NOIR AND BARBERA

---

1 small head radicchio (about 6 ounces)✦

1 tablespoon extra-virgin olive oil, plus ¼ cup

Fine sea salt

2 garlic cloves, thinly sliced

½ teaspoon dried oregano

Two 15-ounce cans cannellini or pinto beans, drained and rinsed

1 cup water

Freshly ground black pepper

1 lemon, cut into wedges

½ cup toasted and crushed hazelnuts

Parmigiano-Reggiano cheese for garnish (optional)

Sourdough or other crusty bread for serving

✦ Treviso radicchio looks like a purple oversize endive, with thinner leaves that are a little more tender than rounder varieties of radicchio. If you find it, use it in this recipe—the tender leaves roast really well. If radicchio isn't available, serve the beans with a few handfuls of peppery arugula on top and opt for a rich white wine instead.

Preheat the oven to 425°F. Line a half-sheet pan with parchment paper or lightly oil it.

Halve the radicchio through its core and cut into six wedges. Put the wedges on the prepared pan and drizzle with the 1 tablespoon oil, then use your hands to mix the oil into the leaves to ensure they are lightly coated. Arrange with a cut side down on the pan and season with a couple of pinches of salt. Roast until the edges crisp up, about 8 minutes.

Meanwhile, in a large saucepan over medium heat, warm the remaining ¼ cup oil. Stir in the garlic and oregano and cook until richly aromatic, 30 seconds to 1 minute. Stir in the beans and water, increase the heat to medium-high, and bring to a simmer, stirring occasionally. Season with pepper and ½ teaspoon salt, then turn the heat to medium-low and simmer, stirring occasionally, until the water mostly evaporates, about 8 minutes, adding more water if the pan looks dry. Mash the beans slightly with a potato masher or a wooden spoon and season with a squeeze or two of lemon. Taste and add more salt if needed. Cover and keep warm.

Spoon the beans into a warmed serving bowl and put the radicchio on top. Garnish with the crushed hazelnuts and grated cheese, if desired. Slice crusty bread to serve alongside.

ORANGE AND FENNEL PORK LOIN ROAST

This is one of those showstopping dishes that actually isn't all that difficult to make. A pork loin roast cooks fairly quickly in the oven and can be sliced thinly, so people can take a few pieces while grazing or make a sandwich with the fennel and onion, which cook with the pork and absorb its savory juices. If you happen to have made Apple-Ginger Preserves (page 76), serve alongside. Grenache/Garnacha delivers red-fruit flavors backed up with spices such as anise and black pepper, which are natural partners with pork. For a more herbaceous wine, go with a traditional Sangiovese, like Chianti Classico. Or head in a rich white wine direction with cool-climate Chardonnay (which is especially good with the preserves).

SERVES 4 TO 6	SANGIOVESE, GRENACHE/GARNACHA, AND CHARDONNAY

1 teaspoon fennel seeds, coarsely chopped

Kosher salt

½ teaspoon freshly ground black pepper

1 tablespoon finely grated orange zest

1 pork loin roast (2 to 2½ pounds)◆

1 medium yellow or red onion, thinly sliced

1 small fennel bulb, cored and thinly sliced, fronds reserved for garnish (optional)

4 sprigs thyme

2 tablespoons extra-virgin olive oil

½ cup white wine or lighter-style red wine

◆ Ask a butcher to tie the roast for you with twine, if possible, so it keeps its shape while cooking. If the roast comes in netting, remove it before cooking the pork so it doesn't interfere with searing. Pork loin roasts are not interchangeable with pork blade roasts, which come from the shoulder of the pig and tend to need at least a couple of hours of roasting until they become tender. They are delicious, though. Molly Stevens's cookbook *All About Roasting* includes all the instructions you need to make a great pork blade roast.

In a small bowl, mix together the fennel seeds, 1½ teaspoons salt, the pepper, and orange zest. Rub the pork with the seasoning mixture, place on a plate, cover loosely with plastic wrap, and refrigerate overnight, or let sit at room temperature while the oven preheats (up to 1 hour). If refrigerating, remove the meat from the refrigerator 1 hour before roasting.

Preheat the oven to 400°F. Put the onion, sliced fennel, and thyme in a roasting pan or Dutch oven that will fit the roast snuggly. Mix in 1 tablespoon of the oil and a pinch of salt and spread the vegetables in an even layer.

In a large sauté pan over medium-high heat, warm the remaining 1 tablespoon oil. Sear the pork, turning with tongs to brown all sides and lowering the heat if parts of the pan are scorching, until evenly browned, 6 to 8 minutes. Transfer the pork to the roasting pan. Pour the wine into the sauté pan, bring to a boil over high heat, and cook, scraping the bottom of the pan with a wooden spoon to dislodge any browned bits, until the wine is reduced by half, about 2 minutes. Pour the wine over the pork.

Roast the pork until an instant-read thermometer inserted into the thickest part of the roast reaches 140° to 145°F, 45 minutes to 1 hour (if your roast is on the small side, start checking after 40 minutes). Let the pork rest in the pan for 15 to 20 minutes before slicing to allow it to reabsorb its juices. Discard the thyme.

Slice the pork thinly and serve on top of the vegetables. Garnish with fennel fronds, if desired.

BIG RED WINES

SAVORY CHEDDAR SHORTBREAD 140

ONION JAM 142

ROSEMARY-ROASTED TRI-TIP 143

TATTOOED POTATOES 147

ITALIAN SAUSAGES WITH ROASTED
CAULIFLOWER AND GREENS 148

When you first get into tasting wine, it's easy to fall in love with big red wines, the kind that hit all the right notes in your mouth and leave behind a little sweetness (even though you'd never call them *sweet* wines). And then you meet some wine experts who steer you to the leaner, more mineral-filled wines, and your palate and what you like to drink evolves. With all that said, there's absolutely a place for well-made big reds, especially with robust, smoky, or grilled food. Serve big red wines at a cool room temperature.

CABERNET SAUVIGNON

When I worked in the Napa Valley as a line cook, I passed a sea of Cabernet vines every day on my way to the restaurant. The grapes thrived in the warm, sunny valley, and day-trippers from San Francisco loved their rich, big taste. But as the prices climbed for these wines, my landlord worried about the Cabernet monoculture surrounding his property. Could one virus wipe everything out? It had happened before—in the early twentieth century, most of Europe's vineyard land was destroyed by phylloxera, an insect brought over from America. (For that reason, most vines today are grafted onto American rootstock, which resists the disease.) My landlord's small rebellion against the Napa Cabernet juggernaut was drinking jug wine from the grocery store. The politics of Cabernet can be complicated and the prices steep.

Back to the grape: Cabernet Sauvignon is the offspring of Cabernet Franc and Sauvignon Blanc. It's a sun-loving vine that became the main grape in Bordeaux, where it was blended with Merlot, Cabernet Franc, Malbec, and Petit Verdot. Bordeaux may have been the original cult wine thanks to the British, who bestowed a classification system on their beloved clarets (Bordeaux-blend wines). This officially defined the best areas for winemaking, allowing higher prices for wine produced in specific places. A couple of centuries later and this grading system is still reflected in the prices of prized bottles. Apart from France and California, Cab also grows well in Washington State and parts of Chile, Argentina, Italy, and Australia. Some of the best Cabs and Cab blends show restraint with oak and sweetness, allowing acidity to come through with hits of some combination of cassis, black cherry, plum, fennel, and cocoa powder or coffee. California Cab doesn't need food to complete it, but when you're in the mood for a wine that's rich, chewy, and filled with black currants and even baking spices—and you're eating steak, lamb chops, or roasted porcini mushrooms seasoned with black pepper and fresh herbs—it's hard to go wrong. If you like the black cherry–spicy tannic richness of Cab, look for Ribera del Duero, a red from Spain made predominantly with Tempranillo grapes.

MALBEC

You know when you discover a celebrity's birth name and think, "I can see why they changed it"? That's the case with Malbec. Long before it discovered fame in Argentina as Malbec, it was a local French grape called Côt. It was brought to Argentina's Mendoza region in the nineteenth century before the phylloxera bug had infected the majority of Europe's vineyards. Still, it's pretty amazing how a grape better known for blending into Bordeaux became emblematic of the Argentinian wine industry. Widely available and affordable, these round, sunny wines are just the thing for backyard grilling. But don't ignore the really good, distinctive Malbec that may cost a little more. Made from grapes grown in rocky terrain at higher altitudes (sometimes as high as 5,000 feet above sea level) and harvested by hand, these wines lose some of their generous berry jam qualities and gain an earthy edge. They are still mouth-filling but can make you pause a bit to appreciate them. With Malbec, grilled red meat or mushrooms are a perfect match. Serve some herby chimichurri on the side and you're in business. If you are curious about other South American wines, try Tannat, a tannic, smoky wine from Uruguay, or País, a much lighter red from Chile.

MERLOT

Next to straight-laced Cab, Merlot is the easygoing sibling. The grapes need sun, but they're not sun-obsessive like Cabernet. Merlot also ripens a little earlier, which is why the two complement each other. One vineyard can be harvested before the other is ready to go. Because of its international popularity, Merlot is planted all over the place and produced in large quantities, yet it's also sneakily one of the most valuable grapes, making up the majority of some of the world's most expensive wines in Bordeaux. While it's often blended in France, Merlot, on its own, is round and rich, with a minty black cherry–mocha vibe. Like all

grapes, it can be forgettable when made by industrial-size wineries, but it's precisely Merlot's uncoolness that makes me think it's on the verge of becoming cool again. At the table, Merlot is a great burger or barbecued-chicken wine, though it's not all that friendly with spicy dishes. Merlot is also a great training wine to help you understand the difference between so-called old-world and new-world styles. Pick not-too-expensive bottles from France, Washington State, and California. Put them in paper bags so you can't see the labels and taste them, noting which ones were most fruit-forward and which felt more restrained. Which wines did you like the best? Why did you like them? Did they match with the general new-world and old-world style descriptions (see page 13)? If you enjoy the brambly smoothness of Merlot, then seek out Malbec. If you like the sterner side of Merlot, look for Bordeaux blends.

SYRAH

Not to anthropomorphize too much, but to me, Syrah is the person at the party who skips small talk and goes straight to the intense deep-dive of a conversation. This is a black olive, bacon, and black pepper kind of wine. At home in the Rhône Valley but also grown elsewhere in France as well as in California, Washington State, South Africa, Australia, and South America, these wines can be brooding and leathery but also bold and sometimes even jammy. The most serious and expensive Syrah is in the Northern Rhône wines from Côte-Rôtie and Hermitage. Around the Rhône Valley, Syrah is often blended with Grenache and Mourvèdre for lighter, easier, and affordable Côte du Rhône wines and used in rich and jammy (and expensive) Châteauneuf-du-Pape. In Australia, where the grape has grown since the nineteenth century and is called Shiraz, it's big, oaked, and inky, with notes of blackberries and lavender. Syrah made in a more natural style can still be sunny and rich but is often lighter in body and alcohol than classic Syrah or Shiraz. Bold Syrah is a natural fit with bold food. It's perfect with red meat, like lamb with garlic and rosemary. Because of its black pepper and black olive spiciness, it can also work with mezze spreads filled with cumin, cilantro, eggplant, tomatoes, feta cheese, and kebabs, as well as complex layered north Indian dishes. If you like Syrah, try Bandol Rouge, a wild, deep red from Provence made with the Mourvèdre grape.

ZINFANDEL

To me, Zinfandel is the ultimate California grape, emblematic of a state that's a little goofy or loud at times but also open-minded and adaptable. Plus, the old Zin vines around the city of Lodi (where the grape has been grown since long before Prohibition) are downright gnarly. When I was a high school student in California, a wine newsletter arrived in the mail describing a "Cab man" as someone who didn't eat quiche and a "Zin dude" as someone who not only ate quiche but also had a great recipe for quiche. (I think the implication was that a guy who liked Zinfandel wasn't afraid that making quiche would challenge his manhood—this was a lifetime ago in the understanding of gender-normative behaviors.) For years, Zinfandel became so big that you could sip only a small glass of it before you were knocked out with its sky-high alcohol—sometimes as high as 17 percent (other rich reds contain around 14 percent).

Fortunately, Zin is reinventing itself again, becoming lighter but still exuberant, filled with blackberry and spice. In the hands of the next generation of winemakers, it has also been transformed into a fruity, savory, light wine with the help of carbonic maceration, the method used in Beaujolais Nouveau (see Gamay, page 107). When talking classic, big Zinfandel, it's hard to find a better wine to serve with a rich, chocolate-imbued Mexican mole (Zinfandel plays up the flavors of cocoa and chiles). If you like your barbecue with a smoky sauce, Zinfandel also has your back. Any Zin fan should try Primitivo, the Italian genetic twin, to compare different wines from the same family tree. For those seeking out another spicy, bold wine, look for California Carignan (also spelled Carignane).

SAVORY CHEDDAR SHORTBREAD

If you've ever been a fan of Cheez-It crackers, these shortbread are the DIY alternative. I encountered this recipe while writing a story for the *San Francisco Chronicle* about Sue Conley and Peggy Smith, the founders of Cowgirl Creamery. Sue said her mother always topped them with pecans and cooled them on paper bags to soak up any oil left after baking. I've made a few minor changes, but the sharp Cheddar bite in each shortbread is true to the source of inspiration. A quick note on the recipe: Use a stand mixer—it's not easy to mix the dough by hand. Also, be sure to use the "scoop and sweep" method of measuring flour (see Baking, page 30). Cheddar and big red wines have long been friends; everything from Merlot and Bordeaux to Zinfandel works well with the nutty, rich flavors of the cheese.

MAKES ABOUT 24 SHORTBREAD	MERLOT, CABERNET SAUVIGNON, AND ZINFANDEL

¾ cup plus 1 tablespoon (116 g) all-purpose flour

¼ cup (18 g) almond flour or meal*

½ teaspoon kosher salt

½ teaspoon paprika

¼ teaspoon baking powder

8 tablespoons (1 stick) (113 g) unsalted butter, at room temperature

8 ounces (225 g) Cheddar cheese, preferably sharp, grated with the medium holes of a box grater

In a medium bowl, whisk together both flours, the salt, paprika, and baking powder. Set aside.

In the bowl of a stand mixer fitted with the paddle attachment, beat the butter on medium speed until smooth, 2 to 3 minutes. Turn the speed to low and add the cheese in handfuls, beating a few times after each addition, until it's all thoroughly mixed in, about 3 minutes, stopping to scrape down the sides of the bowl with a rubber spatula as needed. With the mixer on low speed, gradually add the flour mixture until

incorporated. The dough will be stiff, so let the mixer use its muscle to get the job done. If it is still crumbly, press the dough into the base of the bowl with your hands to help it come together.

Lay a sheet of parchment paper on a work surface. Scrape the dough onto the paper and form into a log about 12 inches long. Wrap the log snugly in the paper, twisting the ends tightly. (If you don't have parchment paper, wrap the log in plastic wrap.) Refrigerate for at least 2 hours or up to overnight.

Preheat the oven to 375°F. Unwrap the dough and use the parchment paper to line a half-sheet pan. Line another half-sheet pan with parchment paper. (If not using parchment paper, lightly oil the pans.) Slice the dough crosswise into 24 coins just under ½ inch thick and divide between the pans, spacing the coins about 2 inches apart.

Bake the dough, rotating the pans halfway through, until the shortbread are golden brown along the edges, 14 to 16 minutes. Let cool completely on the pans. The shortbread can be stored in an airtight container at room temperature for up to 2 weeks.

* If you don't have almond flour, use an additional 1½ tablespoons all-purpose flour.

ONION JAM

The perfect condiment with tangy rich cheeses, slices of steak, or a bit of pâté, a good onion jam (pictured at right on page 145) can outperform its humble appearance. With beef or lamb roasted with rosemary and garlic and served with a glass of Syrah or Zinfandel, the jam shines as a simple counterpoint that won't detract from the other hard-hitting flavors. It's extra-good the next day with leftovers in a sandwich.

MAKES ABOUT 1 CUP | SYRAH AND ZINFANDEL

2 tablespoons extra-virgin olive oil

2 medium yellow onions, thinly sliced

¼ cup granulated sugar

¼ cup red wine vinegar

1 tablespoon fresh thyme leaves, or 1 teaspoon dried thyme

½ teaspoon kosher salt

¼ teaspoon freshly ground black pepper

Have a heatproof 1-cup jar and lid ready.

In a medium saucepan over medium heat, warm the oil. Add the onions and cook, stirring occasionally, until golden brown, 12 to 15 minutes. If the onions start to burn in places, turn the heat to medium-low. If you turn your back for a few minutes and the pan starts to brown too quickly, add a splash of water and stir with a wooden spoon to dislodge some of the browned bits from the pan.

Turn the heat to low, sprinkle the sugar over the onions, and let it melt without stirring, about 1 minute. Stir the onions, increase the heat to medium, and cook until the onions turn a deep golden-amber color, about 2 minutes. Pour in the vinegar and cook, stirring, until most of the vinegar has evaporated, about 2 minutes more. Stir in the thyme, salt, and pepper.

Spoon the onion jam into the jar. Let sit, uncovered, at room temperature until cool, then screw on the lid and store in the refrigerator for up to 1 month.

ROSEMARY-ROASTED TRI-TIP

There's a reason steak house wine lists go deep on Cabernet Sauvignon. Take a steak, dust it with crushed black peppercorns, and it's going to be a hit with a classic bottle of red, especially one that comes with tongue-smacking tannins that help cut through the richness of the meat. In other words, there's no reason to mess with a proven match. Instead, I'm rethinking steak house portions, roasting a larger cut in the oven with the idea that it can be served sliced for sharing. It also opens up the opportunity to try out other mouth-filling reds, such as Syrah or Zinfandel. Tri-tip is a favorite of mine: the West Coast cut roasts well and has that perfect balance of meaty flavor and juicy texture—as long as it's not overcooked. (Marinating it in a prune-garlic puree overnight yields even juicier meat.) Adding rosemary sprigs underneath the meat gently perfumes it as it roasts. To complete the meal, serve with Tattooed Potatoes (page 147), Onion Jam (facing page), and romaine hearts mixed with Green Goddess Dressing (see page 59).

SERVES 6 | SYRAH/SHIRAZ, ZINFANDEL, RIOJA, AND CABERNET SAUVIGNON

---

5 pitted prunes

2 garlic cloves, minced

2 tablespoons extra-virgin olive oil

1 tablespoon balsamic vinegar

1½ teaspoons kosher salt

1 tri-tip roast (about 2 pounds)*

4 sprigs rosemary

¾ teaspoon freshly ground black pepper

½ small head escarole, cored and leaves separated (optional)

Flaky sea salt

The day before cooking, put the prunes in a small bowl and cover with hot tap water. Let sit for 5 minutes, then drain, saving the soaking water. In a mini food processor or a blender, combine the prunes, garlic, 1 tablespoon of the oil, the vinegar, kosher salt, and 2 tablespoons of the soaking water and blend until this marinade is nearly smooth.

Put the tri-tip in a ziplock bag and add the marinade, letting it thoroughly coat the meat on all sides. Add one of the rosemary sprigs, seal the bag, and refrigerate overnight.

Remove the meat from the refrigerator about 1 hour before cooking. Then, 30 minutes before cooking, preheat the oven to 400°F.

Line a half-sheet pan with parchment paper and put the remaining three rosemary sprigs in the center. Remove the meat from the marinade, wipe off the excess marinade with a paper towel, and place the meat on top of the rosemary. Season with the pepper.

CONTINUED

ROSEMARY-ROASTED TRI-TIP, CONTINUED

Roast the tri-tip until an instant-read thermometer inserted into the center of the meat reaches 125°F for medium-rare and 135°F for medium, about 30 minutes. (Start checking after 25 minutes.) Let the meat rest for 10 to 15 minutes before carving—when fresh out of the oven, it's still cooking, and cutting into it too soon causes it to lose a lot of flavorful juices.

While the meat rests, if using, spread the escarole leaves out on a half-sheet pan, rub with the remaining 1 tablespoon oil, and season with a pinch of kosher salt. Arrange the leaves so they lie flat and don't overlap too much, then roast until browned in places, 8 to 10 minutes. Let cool on the pan.

Find the grain of the tri-tip (the direction the meat fibers are running) and slice against it, starting at the smallest tip end and working along the length of the meat (this ensures the meat will be more tender to eat). Lay the escarole leaves on a large plate or platter and put the meat on top. Offer flaky sea salt on the side for seasoning.

+ Tri-tip can easily be larger or smaller than 2 pounds, and butchers occasionally cut it into smaller steaks. If using a tri-tip larger than 2 pounds, go by the internal temperature to tell when the roast is done; for smaller pieces, anticipate a shorter cooking time. On the West Coast, tri-tip is a favorite cut for grilling, so feel free to cook the marinated meat on the grill instead. Put the meat over a medium-hot fire and add the rosemary sprigs next to the meat. Leave the meat for 4 to 5 minutes, then move to a cooler part of the grill (or turn the heat to low), cover the grill, and cook, turning the meat with tongs every 5 minutes, until an instant-read thermometer inserted into the center of the tri-tip reaches 125°F for medium-rare, and 135°F for medium, about 30 minutes. (Start checking after 25 minutes.) Add the escarole leaves to the grill at the very end to briefly char.

TATTOOED POTATOES

The year my mom discovered Peggy Knickerbocker's book *Olive Oil from Tree to Table* was the year tattooed potatoes became part of our family's repertoire. More than two decades later, I'm still impressed by the results of baking potatoes cut-sides down so that herbs adhere to the crispy potato pieces like tattoos. The original recipe, which ran in *Gourmet* magazine a few decades ago, used a lot of butter, but Knickerbocker's take with olive oil makes this recipe an easier sell for everyday cooking. Over the years, our family has tinkered with just about every potato variety, and the good news is that nearly any will work, save for very fresh new potatoes, which are not starchy enough to cling to the herbs. Serve these potatoes with grilled steak and Cabernet Sauvignon, Merlot, or a Bordeaux blend for a modern take on steak house classics. Or, frankly, serve them to anyone who loves potatoes.

SERVES 4 | ANY RED WINE

2 tablespoons extra-virgin olive oil

1 pound small red potatoes, halved lengthwise

¼ teaspoon kosher salt

Herb sprigs (such as flat-leaf parsley, rosemary, and/or thyme)

Flaky sea salt

Preheat the oven to 425°F. Spread 1 tablespoon of the oil in a roasting pan or on a quarter-sheet (9 by 13-inch) pan.✦

In a large bowl, mix together the potatoes, the remaining 1 tablespoon oil, and the kosher salt. For each potato half, trim an herb sprig so it fits onto the cut side of a potato and press to adhere. Place the potato, cut-side down, in the prepared pan. Repeat with the remaining potato halves and herb sprigs. (The idea is that the herb will "tattoo" itself to the potato as it cooks in the olive oil.)

Roast the potatoes until the centers are tender when pierced with a fork and the skin around the edges of the potatoes begins to look wrinkled and golden brown, 35 to 40 minutes depending on the size of the potatoes. (It is better to err on roasting them longer.)

Remove the potatoes from the oven and allow them to rest for a few minutes to absorb any extra oil. Using a metal spatula, pry the potatoes from the pan if they are sticking so that the golden-brown crust and the herbs stay in place. Serve herb-side up, with flaky sea salt on the side.

✦ You can use a glass baking dish to roast the potatoes, which allows you to peek at the bottom to see if they are browning. I prefer metal because I've found that glass can minimize how crisp I can get the potatoes, but that could entirely be on my oven.

ITALIAN SAUSAGES WITH ROASTED CAULIFLOWER AND GREENS

Roasting sausages in the oven with vegetables is a simple way to capture their savory juices so they can permeate the other food in the pan. Cauliflower, red onion, and capers are always a winning combination when roasted, and the hearty sausages complete the meal. There's no shortage of red wines that pair well with this dish, but those with sunny dispositions, like Argentine Malbec or the Grenache, Syrah, and Mourvèdre blends of the southern Rhône Valley, have a juicy quality that matches well with the sweetness of the caramelized cauliflower and sausages.

SERVES 4 | MALBEC, MERLOT, AND CÔTES DU RHÔNE

---

1 small head cauliflower, cut into florets (about 4 cups), large pieces halved or quartered

½ medium red onion, sliced into ¼- to ½-inch pieces

2 tablespoons capers, drained

¼ teaspoon red pepper flakes

Kosher salt

3 tablespoons extra-virgin olive oil

1 pound hot or sweet fresh Italian sausages (about 4 links)

5 cups packed baby spinach (4 to 5 ounces) *

1 lemon (optional)

* In place of the spinach, you can use 1 bunch chard or kale or 5 cups mixed braising greens. Slice the stems thinly and the leaves slightly thicker, then cook in a pot of salted water until softened, 2 to 3 minutes. Drain and stir into the cauliflower once the sausages are done. Roast in place of the spinach for a few minutes in the oven until the greens have softened a bit more.

Preheat the oven to 450°F.

In a large bowl, mix together the cauliflower, onion, capers, red pepper flakes, and ¼ teaspoon salt. Add the oil and mix to coat the vegetables well.

Heat a half-sheet pan or 7-quart Dutch oven in the oven for 2 to 3 minutes. Remove the pan and add the cauliflower mixture. Return the pan to the oven and roast until the florets just start to brown, about 5 minutes. Remove the pan and add the sausages, arranging them so they touch the base of the pan and aren't on top of the cauliflower pieces. Return the pan to the oven and roast, turning the sausages over once, until the cauliflower has caramelized and the sausages feel firm and are cooked through (the juices should run clear when the sausages are pierced with a fork), 15 to 20 minutes.

Transfer the sausages to a cutting board, let them rest, and then slice, if desired. Add the spinach to the pan and stir into the cauliflower to wilt. If the spinach isn't wilting quickly, return the pan to the oven for a minute and try again. Zest half of the lemon over the vegetables, if desired, and taste, seasoning with a pinch of salt.

Serve the sausages on top of the vegetables. Cut a wedge out of the lemon, if using, and squeeze it over the top.

SWEET WINES

BAKED PEACHES WITH COCONUT
AND SLICED ALMONDS 154

SWEET FOCACCIA WITH FRUIT 157

AGED PARMIGIANO-REGGIANO
WITH PEARS AND HONEY 159

ALMOND AND OLIVE OIL BISCOTTI 160

CHOCOLATE OLIVE OIL CAKE 162

This chapter is all about making a case for sweet wines, which are simultaneously some of the most beguiling, historic, and misunderstood wines in the world. If a wine is sweet, it's often because some of the grape sugars remain after the wine is fermented (see Sweetness, page 165). That being said, the sweet-wine category is quite broad, with rarefied examples such as Sauternes in France and Tokaji Aszú in Hungary offering layered, honeyed sweetness, while lightly sweet sparkling wines, like Moscato d'Asti, are refreshing, affordable low-alcohol palate cleansers. All are worth exploring. Serve most dessert wines slightly chilled unless instructed otherwise.

APPASSIMENTO

Drying various combinations of Moscato, Malvasia, Trebbiano, and other local grapes before pressing has given the world Italy's passito wines. These wines are delicate and fragrant all at once, with any combination of flavors ranging from candied orange, orange blossom, and honeysuckle to dried fig, tropical fruit, and golden raisins. This is all thanks to the appassimento process, which involves picking grapes and laying them out on mats to partially dry. In the old days, the drying happened in the sun, but today many winemakers prefer appassimento forzato, in which the grapes dry in temperature- and humidity-controlled rooms for consistency. It used to be quite common for Italian winemaking families to produce wines in the appassimento style, but because of the extra labor and cost involved, the younger generations would rather create something else. Which is why I'm always worried that as more producers stop making them, the export market will disappear,

the local market will follow, and we'll forget all about these historic and beautiful wines. Maybe I'm being dramatic, but still: if you see a bottle, go for it. Drink appassimento wines with simple, not-too-sweet treats, like almond biscotti.

FORTIFIED WINES

Port, Madeira, Marsala, and Banyuls are fortified wines made sweet by adding a distilled spirit, like brandy, to halt fermentation before all the grape sugars are consumed by yeast. That's a clinical way of describing some of the most historic wines in the world. The British had a lot to do with spreading their popularity. When Napoleon was busy conquering the Italian peninsula in the early nineteenth century, the British navy protected Sicily, persuading the Sicilians to accept a constitution and parliament. While that didn't quite stick, the British also established the Marsala wine industry and solidified a market for fortified wines back in England. In the United States, it's largely thanks to the influence of Madeira that Chief Justice John Marshall was able to establish the principle of separation of powers—he plied everyone with good-quality Madeira until they agreed with him. These wines were popular far from their origins thanks to their higher alcohol levels and sticky sweetness, which allowed them to withstand transport and have a long shelf life. While Portugal's Madeira and port fall on the richer side of the fortified-wine spectrum, Banyuls from the South of France tends to be lighter and less dense. Meanwhile, Marsala is somewhere in between. Not all fortified wines are sweet. For instance, sherry is fermented dry before being fortified and, although some fortified sherry is sweet, the vast majority is completely dry. (If you like dry sherry, you may also like orange wines.) I find chocolate to be a hard pairing with most wines, but port and Madeira are able to match the richness and sweetness while adding acidity, almost like eating dried fruit with chocolate.

LATE-HARVEST WINES

As the name suggests, late-harvest wines ("vendage tardive" in French and "vendemmia tardiva" in Italian) are made from grapes harvested late in the year, mostly in cooler regions. While harvest for dry wines starts as early as August, grapes for late-harvest wines cling to the vines late into fall, risking contact with rain, hail, and other elements for several more weeks than most sane winemakers can stand. So why do it? For the honeyed richness layered with acidity and notes of everything from pineapple to hazelnut, pear, and dried apricot. Semillon, Chenin Blanc, Riesling, Muscat/Moscato, and Gewürztraminer are all often used for late-harvest wines. These wines are classic matches with triple-crème cheeses and fresh or caramelized fruits, such as roast peaches or roast pineapple.

Under this late-harvest umbrella, production is even trickier for the following wines:

Botrytis: While most farmers want to avoid rot and fungus, botrytis is the key to the great wines of Sauternes (made mainly with Sauvignon Blanc and Semillon), Tokaji (made with Furmint and other Hungarian grapes), and certain late-harvest German Rieslings (such as TBA, or trockenbeerenauslese). Also called noble rot, botrytis cinera is a fungus

that dries out grapes and concentrates their sugars while they are still on the vine, yielding wines filled with honeyed lushness and a faint waxy earthiness. For lovers of Mexican cooking, botrytis is the grape equivalent of the corn fungus huitlacoche.

Ice Wine ("Eiswein" in German): An even more extreme example of late-harvest processes, ice wine is made by letting grapes freeze on the vine before harvest, which causes the sugars to concentrate while preserving acidity. If harvesting grapes stricken with fungus sounds tricky, picking and crushing frozen grapes requires next-level heartiness. Ice wine is a specialty of Canada (primarily Ontario and British Columbia), though it's also made in New York's Finger Lakes region, Michigan, and (to a much lesser extent) Germany—when the weather allows.

SPARKLING MOSCATO

The trend in sparkling wines is to be bone dry, with terms such as "brut zéro," "brut nature," or "non-dosé" to indicate no extra sweetness has been added. But not all sparkling wines are meant to be enjoyed this way. Take Moscato d'Asti, a gently fizzy, low-alcohol sparkler that's quite refreshing. Made in Piedmont, the land of Nebbiolo, Moscato d'Asti is easygoing and lightly sweet—the kind of thing to drink if you need a break from serious red wine. Sparkling Moscato wines from Asti or elsewhere in northern Italy remind me of peaches with yogurt—a little tangy and fuzzy with peachy–orange blossom aromas. At 5 or 6 percent alcohol, they offer delicate sweetness after a meal.

BAKED PEACHES WITH COCONUT AND SLICED ALMONDS

The first thing to understand about Moscato (also called Muscat Moscatel and Muskateller) is that it's not just a grape but an entire grape family that branches out with aunts, uncles, and cousins all over the world. The matriarch of the family—the one you'll most likely encounter—is Moscato Bianco, which is made in a range of styles. In northern Italy, it's mostly known for making popular sweet sparkling wines such as Moscato d'Asti, which has gentle bubbles and peaches-and-cream aromas. If you have that one perfect peach on hand, you could just slice it, pour sparkling Moscato over it, and eat it as a really simple dessert. Or take it to the next level and roast the peaches with honey, coconut, and almonds. Even so-so peaches are transformed into something memorable when prepared this way.

SERVES 4 | MOSCATO D'ASTI AND DRY OR DEMI-SEC PROSECCO

---

4 ripe peaches, halved and pitted

2 tablespoons honey

¼ cup unsweetened coconut flakes

¼ cup sliced almonds

Preheat the oven to 400°F. Line an 8-inch square baking pan with parchment paper or aluminum foil (baked-on peach juice is hard to clean).

Place the peaches, cut-side up, in the prepared pan. Drizzle with the honey and roast until the peaches start to brown around the edges, about 17 minutes. Remove from the oven and sprinkle the tops with the coconut and almonds. Roast until the peach juices are bubbling and the coconut and almonds are toasted, 3 to 4 minutes more. Serve warm.

SWEET FOCACCIA WITH FRUIT

One of my favorite things about dessert wines is how they can taste as though they contain an extravagant combination of citrus zests, toasted nuts, spices, and wildflowers, all bathed in honey and acidity. This recipe serves as a backdrop to explore dessert wines from outside of Europe, such as late-harvest Gewürztraminer, Moscato, or Semillon from the West Coast, Chile, and Australia, or ice wines from Canada or New York State. Baking fruit on top of focaccia gives the bread a caramelized sweetness that complements late-harvest wines but doesn't outshine them. You can be flexible with the fruit depending on what's in season, from cherries in late spring to sliced peaches, fresh figs, or seedless grapes as the year progresses. Pair with nutty, subtly sweet cheeses, like Cypress Grove's Midnight Moon or aged Gouda.

MAKES TWO 10-INCH FOCACCIA | LATE-HARVEST WINE

---

3 cups plus 2 tablespoons (440 g) all-purpose flour, plus more for dusting

1 teaspoon instant yeast*

1¼ cups (300 ml) room-temperature water

4 tablespoons extra-virgin olive oil, plus more as needed

2 teaspoons kosher salt

2 cups fruit (such as pitted cherries, seedless grapes, sliced peaches, or halved fresh figs)

Generous 1 tablespoon granulated sugar or coarse turbinado sugar

Rosemary sprigs for topping (optional)

Flaky sea salt (optional)

In the bowl of a stand mixer fitted with the paddle attachment, stir together the flour and yeast. Add the water and 1 tablespoon of the oil and beat on low speed until a shaggy dough forms, about 1 minute. Remove the paddle attachment and scrape any bits of dough off the paddle. Cover the bowl with a kitchen towel and let the dough rest for 20 minutes to allow the flour to hydrate.

Remove the towel and attach the dough hook to the mixer. Add the kosher salt and mix the dough on medium speed, stopping to reposition the dough as needed to ensure it kneads evenly on the hook, until smooth, about 4 minutes.

To make the dough by hand, in a large bowl, stir together the flour and yeast, then stir in the water and oil with your hands until a shaggy dough forms. Cover with a kitchen towel and let the dough rest for 20 minutes to allow the flour to hydrate. Dust a work surface lightly with flour, put the dough on top, and sprinkle with the kosher salt, rubbing it into the dough. Knead by pressing the heel of your hand into the dough and dragging it back, repeating this motion until the dough feels smooth to the touch, about 5 minutes.

CONTINUED

SWEET FOCACCIA WITH FRUIT, CONTINUED

Put the dough in a lightly oiled bowl, cover with plastic wrap, and let rise at room temperature until doubled in size, about 2 hours.

Brush a half-sheet pan with 1 tablespoon oil. Dust a work surface generously with flour. Dislodge the dough from the bowl and put it on top of the flour. Cut the dough in half, tuck the cut edge under, and pat each piece into an oval or rectangle 9 or 10 inches long and 7 inches wide, ensuring that the dough doesn't stick to the work surface. Transfer the pieces to the prepared pan, spacing them 1 inch apart. Cover with a towel and let the dough rest for 30 minutes at a warm room temperature. (The top of the dough may get a little dry, but that's okay.)

Using your fingertips, press the dough deeply to form dimples, spaced about ½ inch apart. Cover the dough again with a towel and let rise for 30 minutes at a warm room temperature.

While the dough rises, preheat the oven to 450°F. If using a baking stone,** place it on the center rack of the oven before preheating.

After the dough has risen, put the fruit on top, pressing in the pieces to adhere. Brush the dough with the remaining 2 tablespoons oil and sprinkle with the sugar. If desired, distribute a few rosemary sprigs and a few pinches of flaky salt evenly across the top.

Bake the focaccia until the fruit juices have started to caramelize in places and the edges are golden brown, about 30 minutes. Let the focaccia cool on the pans and then eat warm or at room temperature. Leftover focaccia should be eaten by the next day or frozen for up to 1 month. Reheat frozen focaccia in a 400°F oven until hot.

* Instant yeast doesn't work faster than active dry yeast, but it does work differently: Instead of being hydrated in water before being mixed into the flour, instant yeast can be mixed directly into the flour and will begin to activate once the water is added. If using active dry yeast, dissolve the yeast in the water and let it sit for 5 to 10 minutes before adding it to the flour.

** For more information on using a baking stone, see the note on page 121).

AGED PARMIGIANO-REGGIANO WITH PEARS AND HONEY

My cousin Scott Naylor says one of his most memorable wine-and-food moments came while tasting Sauternes when studying for a sommelier exam. Sauternes is a dessert wine made with grapes infected by botrytis, a fungus that concentrates grape sugars while rotting the bunches (see page 152). While that's not a promising description, the wines that this so-called noble rot helps to create have historically been some of the most valued in the world. In his study materials, Scott read that Sauternes and Brie were a classic match, and so he dug out a nothing-special piece of the creamy cheese from the refrigerator. The result—as he recounts it—was plainly wow. This special golden wine had made ordinary Brie taste like a million bucks.

What does any of this have to do with Parmigiano-Reggiano? Just that serving a single cheese with dessert wine can be special, whether it's a triple-crème cheese with Sauternes; an aged goat cheese with German TBA (trockenbeerenauslese) Riesling, also made with the help of botrytis; Roquefort with Banyuls; or aged Parmigiano-Reggiano with an Italian passito or Vin Santo. The key is buying a good piece of Parmigiano and letting it come to room temperature before you serve it. The more aged the cheese is, the better; most Parmigiano comes to market after aging for 18 months. With a little honey and fresh pears alongside, it's a pretty spectacular way to end the night.

SERVES 3 OR 4 | PASSITO AND VIN SANTO

---

3 to 4 ounces Parmigiano-Reggiano, at room temperature

1 ripe pear (any variety as long as it's ripe; if small, use 2), sliced

Honey for drizzling

Put the piece of cheese on a cutting board with the pear slices. Instead of slicing the cheese, break it into chunks by digging into it with the tip of a blunt knife. Offer honey when serving in case anyone wants to drizzle a little on the cheese or pears.

ALMOND AND OLIVE OIL BISCOTTI

It's a real shame that thoughtful dessert wines, the kind that used to be revered in days of yore, have fallen out of fashion. But there's a reason: they take a long time to make and usually involve letting grapes raisin a bit before pressing. The results are more time and labor but less wine, so it's no wonder that the next generations in the family business are phasing out such wines as Tuscany's Vin Santo or Sicily's famed passito. To me, that's even more of a reason to seek out and try them. One of the best ways to get to know these wines is to serve them with a simple, fennel-infused biscotti. Made with olive oil instead of butter, the biscotti is less sweet and more addictively crunchy, and it allows the wine to be the star.

MAKES ABOUT 20 BISCOTTI | PASSITO AND VIN SANTO

1 cup whole raw almonds

1½ cups (210 g) all-purpose flour, plus more for dusting

¾ cup (150 g) granulated sugar

½ teaspoon baking powder

½ teaspoon fine sea salt or kosher salt

½ teaspoon fennel seeds, coarsely chopped or crushed

1 orange

2 eggs, at room temperature

¼ cup extra-virgin olive oil

Preheat the oven to 350°F. Line a half-sheet pan with parchment paper.

Spread the almonds on the prepared pan and toast until lightly fragrant but not completely toasted through, 10 to 12 minutes. Let the almonds cool for a few minutes, then coarsely chop and set aside. Reserve the pan for baking the biscotti. Keep the oven set at 350°F.

In a large bowl, whisk together the flour, sugar, baking powder, salt, and fennel seeds. Using a Microplane, zest the orange directly over the bowl and stir in the almonds.

In a small bowl, break up the eggs with a fork and stir in the oil until evenly and thoroughly combined. Stir the egg mixture into the flour mixture with a rubber spatula. Use your hands to press the dough into the base of the bowl to bring the dough together.

Dust a work surface lightly with flour and put the dough on top. Using your hands, roll and pat the dough into a log about 12 inches long, dusting with a little flour to prevent sticking. Place the dough on the prepared pan and press down to flatten so it's about 3 inches wide.

Bake the log until the edges are golden and the top only slightly springs back when touched, about 30 minutes. Let cool for 10 minutes on the pan, then carefully transfer to a cutting board. Using your sharpest knife (serrated or plain-edged is fine), slice the log at an angle into ½-inch-thick biscotti. It might be a little crumbly, but that's okay.

Put the biscotti back on the pan (include the end pieces unless you want a snack) with the cut sides facing up and bake for 12 minutes. Remove the pan from the oven and turn each biscotti over (use a spatula if the pieces are too hot to handle). Bake until the cookies feel quite dry and are lightly toasted on the top, about 12 minutes more. Let the biscotti cool completely on the pan. Biscotti can be stored in an airtight container at room temperature for up to 2 weeks.

CHOCOLATE OLIVE OIL CAKE

The olive oil, orange, and prunes in this recipe curb some of the sweetness in a more classic flourless chocolate cake. This makes it a better match with deep-red dessert wines, like port or Banyuls, that can stand up to rich chocolate flavor without faltering. A deep-purple, ripe California Zinfandel may also hold up to the sweetness of chocolate without tasting bitter, but it's not always a sure bet. The sweetness of the wine is subdued next to the cake, but there's an amazing brown sugar–golden raisin taste that lingers long after.

MAKES ONE 8- TO 9-INCH CAKE | PORT AND BANYULS

Unsweetened cocoa powder (either natural or Dutch-processed) for dusting

8 pitted prunes, diced

7 ounces (100 g) bittersweet chocolate (65 to 70% cacao), coarsely chopped

½ cup extra-virgin olive oil (not too green or grassy tasting*), plus more for the pan

1 tablespoon finely grated orange zest

1 tablespoon pure vanilla extract (optional)

3 eggs, separated

½ teaspoon fine sea salt or kosher salt

⅔ cup (130 g) granulated sugar

1 cup (110 g) lightly packed almond flour, whisked to break up any lumps

* See olive oil advice in "Cooking from This Book," page 25.

Preheat the oven to 350°F. Lightly oil a 9-inch round springform pan or an 8-inch square baking pan. Line the base of the springform pan or the bottom and sides of the square pan with parchment paper. Dust the parchment with cocoa powder, shaking out the excess.

Put the prunes in a small heatproof bowl and pour in enough hot tap water to cover (about ½ cup). Let the prunes plump up for 10 minutes, then drain.

In a large microwave-safe bowl, melt the chocolate on half power until completely melted. (Alternatively, melt the chocolate in a large heatproof bowl set over simmering water in a saucepan, taking care that the bowl doesn't touch the water.) Let the chocolate sit for 1 minute, then whisk in the oil, followed by the prunes, orange zest, vanilla (if using), egg yolks, and ¼ teaspoon of the salt.

In the bowl of a stand mixer fitted with the whisk attachment, or in a large bowl using a handheld electric mixer, whip the egg whites and remaining ¼ teaspoon salt on medium-high speed until frothy, about 1 minute. Add the sugar in three additions, whipping in between additions, until the whites form soft ribbons when the whisk is lifted out of the bowl, about 2 minutes. Using a rubber spatula, gently stir the whites into the chocolate mixture in three additions, then gently stir in the almond flour until completely mixed in. Pour the batter into the prepared pan, smoothing out the top with the spatula.

CONTINUED

CHOCOLATE OLIVE OIL CAKE, CONTINUED

Bake the cake until the top is set and shiny and a toothpick or knife inserted into the center has a few wet crumbs attached, 30 to 32 minutes. Remove the cake from the oven and run a paring knife around the edges of the pan. Let cool for 30 minutes on a wire rack, then unmold.

Cut the cake into wedges or squares and serve dusted with cocoa powder for a bittersweet finish.

Sweetness

It's common to hear friends or family members say they only drink dry wine, but there's a lot of gray area in what a dry wine actually is. Technically, "dry" describes a wine that has no discernible sweetness, meaning that during fermentation, yeasts have eaten nearly all the grape sugars so that 0.5 percent or less sugar remains. This is the residual sugar. In some cases, "dry" is written on the label to indicate a wine is not sweet. But "dry" can easily be a misleading description. Some exuberantly aromatic wines, like Muscat or Gewürztraminer, can taste almost sweet even though they're technically dry. At the same time, some wines with high acidity can cover up residual sugar. If the wine is balanced, the sweetness is not noticeable. Although many think that dry wines are a more sophisticated choice, I'm not so convinced. Even brut Champagne has a touch of sugar (called dosage) added to it before bottling, and few people complain that it is too sweet.

ABOUT THE AUTHOR

Kate Leahy is the award-winning author of more than ten books about food and/or wine, including *La Buvette, Lavash,* and *Burma Superstar*. Her *A16 Food + Wine* was the IACP Cookbook of the Year and winner of the Julia Child First Book Award. Kate's recipes and articles have appeared in *EatingWell* and *Smithsonian Magazine* and on websites explorepartsunknown.com and Food52.com. She lives in San Francisco and hopes to one day have a proper porch to host hangout sessions. Find out more at kateleahycooks.com.

ACKNOWLEDGMENTS

It was the strangest of times when I set out to write about wine, food, and—most important—celebrating moments with friends. This makes me even more grateful for all of the people who came together to make my first solo book come to life.

To my agent, Amy Collins, who made this book a reality by sheer determination and belief in the premise and my capability to take it on. Thanks also for understanding the value of small things, like oven-dried grapes.

To my book team, thank you to my editor, Emma Rudolph, who endorsed the idea of the book from the start and thoughtfully nudged the text along the way. To copy editor Kris Balloun, whose incredible eye for detail and practicality made each recipe and story read more clearly. To art director and designer Emma Campion, who took the raw material and turned it into a happy place to spend time. Thanks also to Jane Chinn, Mari Gill, David Hawk, Stephanie Davis, Allison Renzulli, Rachel Markowitz, and Ken DellaPenta for all the work behind the scenes at Ten Speed Press. Finally, thanks to Lorena Jones for giving me my first shot as a solo author.

To my photo team, what an amazing group of pros. When asked to make magic in a bubble, you made it look effortless. To Erin Scott for bringing color and life into my recipes with your photography—you made me want to jump into the scenes and eat the popcorn. To Lillian Kang, who took my recipes—some of which were still very much works in progress—and made them come together in a beautiful way, with Veronica Laramie assisting. To Jillian Knox, Lilah Scott, and Otis Scott, for being such natural models that you made this look like the kind of party I'd crash.

To my food-and-wine brain trust, the people who have inspired me, answered questions, thought through ideas, sent links, and otherwise steered me to new ideas along the way: Jeff Bareilles, Kristin Donnelly, Lori Galvin, Megan Krigbaum, Soma Mukherjee, Andrea Nguyen, Iris Rowlee, and Molly Stevens. Thanks for letting me pick your brains.

To Shelley Lindgren, who let me jump into the deep end of Italian food and wine with her. Grazie mille.

To Scott Naylor, who became a sounding board for much of this book. Cousin, thank you for sharing your deep wine knowledge and for giving many of these recipes a test-run alongside the pairings. Let's have a glass together at the next family reunion.

To my intrepid group of recipe testers, who were thoughtful and thorough with each run-through while also giving me clear feedback: Elisabeth Biebl, Sandy Binder, Grace Bishop, Camille Enriquez, Mary Ann Shattuck, Maureen Sherman, and Kat Silverstein. I hope some of the recipes find their way into your repertoires. And to Ashley Hamik and Cypress Grove for cheese samples.

To Porch Time: Becca Dawson, Maggie Gordon, Samantha Hagar, Robin Hayes, and Jana Scott. We'll always have those original Château Claremont hang-outs, no matter where we live.

To my parents, Kathy and Tom. The best tattooed potatoes and green goddess dressing always come out of your kitchen. I'm so lucky to have family like you.

And to Patrick Kim, even though I know you'll always be more of a beer guy.

INDEX

A

acidity, 7, 22–23
aging, 12, 21
Albariño, 51, 60, 79
almonds
    Goat Cheese with Almonds and
        Dried Cherries, 96
    Toasted Rosemary Almonds, 42
Alpine red wines, 109, 128
anchovies, 28
appassimento, 151
Apple-Ginger Preserves, 76

B

baking, 30
Banyuls, 151
Barbera, 107, 110, 118, 133
beans, 28
    Olive Oil Beans with Green Sauce, 60
    Oven-Baked Chickpea Fries with
        Tangy Dip, 85
    Roasted Edamame, 84
    Roasted Radicchio with Beans, 133
Beaujolais, 107–8
beef
    Rosemary-Roasted Tri-Tip, 143–44
beets
    Beet and Potato Salad with
        Tarragon, 131
    Pickled Baby Beets, 69
black pepper, 26
body, 8
botrytis, 152
Broccolini Pasta, 116

C

Cabbage and Onion Galette,
    Caramelized, 128–29
Cabernet Franc, 99, 113, 123
Cabernet Sauvignon, 137, 140, 143, 147
capers, 28
carbonic maceration, 10
carrots
    Pickled Carrots, 69
    Spiced Carrots and Walnut Sauce, 49
cauliflower
    Cumin-Roasted Cauliflower, 90
    Giardiniera, 114
    Italian Sausages with Roasted
        Cauliflower and Greens, 148
Cava, 36, 41, 42

Champagne, 35, 41, 46
Champagne stoppers, 18
Chardonnay, 65, 74, 79, 80, 100, 134
cheese
    Baked Feta with Olives and Lemon, 54
    Goat Cheese with Almonds and
        Dried Cherries, 96
    pairing wine and, 72–73
    Red Wine Grazing Board, 110–15
    Savory Cheddar Shortbread, 140
    White Wine Cheese Board, 74
Chenin Blanc, 61, 65–66, 89
Cherries, Dried, Goat Cheese with
    Almonds and, 96
chicken, 29
    Ginger Chicken Salad, 62
    A Really Good Pasta Salad, 93
    Roasted Chicken Legs with Lemon,
        Radishes, and Capers, 80
    Roasted Chipotle Chicken Thighs, 103
Chickpea Fries, Oven-Baked, with
    Tangy Dip, 85
Coconut Curry with Tofu and Braising
    Greens, 61
col fondo, 39
corkscrews, 18
Côtes du Rhône, 115, 148
Crackers, Sea Salt, 56
Crémant, 36
curry powder, 26

D

Dal, Kerala-Inspired, 89
Dolcetto, 107, 110
dry wines, 165

E

earthiness, 10
Edamame, Roasted, 84
Eggplant Lahmajoon, 118–21
Eggs, Harissa Deviled, 45
espumosos, 39

F

Falanghina Flegra, 79
Fiano, 67
filtering, 15
fining, 15
fish
    Chilled Smoked Salmon Spaghetti
        with Capers and Avocado, 46

Oil-Packed Tuna with Potatoes, Olives,
    and Lemon, 79
Poached Salmon with Fennel-Celery
    Salad and Caper Mayo, 100–102
floral accents, 11
food, pairing wine with, 22–23
fortified wines, 151–52
Franciacorta, 36, 41, 42
Frappato, 114
fruitiness, 10

G

Galette, Caramelized Cabbage and
    Onion, 128–29
Gamay, 85, 93, 107–8, 110, 114
Garganega, 67
Garnacha/Grenache, 115, 118, 123,
    131, 134
Gewürztraminer, 66, 74, 90
Giardiniera, 114
glassware, 18
Grapes, Oven-Roasted, 77
Green Goddess Veg Board, 59
Grenache. See Garnacha/Grenache
Grüner Veltliner, 51, 59, 62

H

Harissa Deviled Eggs, 45
herbal accents, 11
herbs, 26

I

ice wine, 152
Italian Sausages with Roasted
    Cauliflower and Greens, 148

J

jams and preserves
    Apple-Ginger Preserves, 76
    Onion Jam, 142

K

Kerala-Inspired Dal, 89

L

Lahmajoon, Eggplant, 118–21
Lamb Meatballs with Yogurt Sauce, 104
Lambrusco, 38, 41, 49, 84
late-harvest wines, 152, 157
lentils
    Kerala-Inspired Dal, 89

M

Madeira, 151, 152, 162
Malbec, 118, 137–38, 148
malo (malolactic fermentation), 8
Marsala, 151
Meatballs, Lamb, with Yogurt Sauce, 104
Merlot, 138, 140, 147, 148
minerality, 11
Montepulciano, 108, 113, 116
Moscato d'Asti, 152, 154
Muscadet, 51, 54
mushrooms
  Garlicky Marinated Mushrooms, 126
  powder, 26

N

natural wine, 14–15
Nebbiolo, 124, 126
Negroamaro, 116
nuts
  buying, 28
  toasting, 28
  See also individual nuts

O

oils, 25
olives, 28
  Baked Feta with Olives and Lemon, 54
  Green Olive Tapenade, 115
  Oil-Packed Tuna with Potatoes,
    Olives, and Lemon, 79
onions
  Caramelized Cabbage and Onion
    Galette, 128–29
  Onion Jam, 142
Orange and Fennel Pork Loin Roast, 134
orange wines, 73, 83, 84, 85, 89, 90,
    93, 131
oven temperatures, 30

P

pans, 30
paprika, 26
passito, 151, 159, 160
pasta, 28–29
  Broccolini Pasta, 116
  Chilled Smoked Salmon Spaghetti
    with Capers and Avocado, 46
  A Really Good Pasta Salad, 93
Pecorino, 67
Peperonata, 113
pét nat, 39, 41, 45, 49
pickles
  Giardiniera, 114
  making, 68
  pairing wine and, 68

Pickled Baby Beets, 69
  Pickled Carrots, 69
Pinot Blanc/Pinot Bianco, 52
Pinot Grigio/Pinot Gris, 52
Pinot Noir, 124–25, 128, 133
Popcorn Four Ways, 40–41
Pork Loin Roast, Orange and Fennel, 134
port, 151, 152, 162
potatoes
  Beet and Potato Salad with
    Tarragon, 131
  Oil-Packed Tuna with Potatoes,
    Olives, and Lemon, 79
  Tattooed Potatoes, 147
pots, 30
Primitivo, 116
Prosecco, 38, 41, 45, 61, 154

R

Radicchio, Roasted, with Beans, 133
red pepper flakes, 26
red wines
  big, 73, 137–39
  picnic, 73, 107–9
  reasonably serious, 73, 123–25
  Red Wine Grazing Board, 110–15
Riesling, 52–53, 61, 62, 74
Rioja, 125, 126, 143
rosé wines, 41, 42, 46, 73, 95, 96, 99,
    100, 103, 104, 118

S

salads
  Beet and Potato Salad with
    Tarragon, 131
  Ginger Chicken Salad, 62
  Poached Salmon with Fennel-Celery
    Salad and Caper Mayo, 100–102
  A Really Good Pasta Salad, 93
salmon
  Chilled Smoked Salmon Spaghetti
    with Capers and Avocado, 46
  Poached Salmon with Fennel-Celery
    Salad and Caper Mayo, 100–102
salt, 23, 25
Sangiovese, 113, 125, 134
Sausages, Italian, with Roasted
    Cauliflower and Greens, 148
Sauvignon Blanc, 53, 54, 59, 62
seasonings, 26
sheet pans, 30
sherry, 151
Shiraz. *See* Syrah/Shiraz
Shortbread, Savory Cheddar, 140
sparkling wines, 35–39, 72
spices, 23, 26

spumante, 39
Squash Wedges, Roasted, 99
sulfites, 14
sur lie, 8
sweetness, 37, 165
sweet wines, 23, 73, 151–52
Syrah/Shiraz, 104, 138–39, 142, 143

T

tannins, 7
Tapenade, Green Olive, 115
Timorasso, 67
tofu, 29
  Coconut Curry with Tofu and
    Braising Greens, 61
Trento, 36
Tuna, Oil-Packed, with Potatoes,
    Olives, and Lemon, 79

V

Valpolicella, 108, 131
vegetables
  Green Goddess Veg Board, 59
  See also individual vegetables
Verdicchio, 67, 80
Vermentino, 51, 60
vinegar, 28–29
Vinho Verde, 41, 53, 60
Vin Santo, 159, 160
Viognier, 66, 80

W

Walnut Sauce, Spiced Carrots and, 49
white wines
  crisp, 51–53, 72
  rich, 65–67, 73
  White Wine Cheese Board, 74
wine
  aging, 12, 21
  buying, 16–17
  for cooking, 29
  and food, 22–23
  opening, 18
  storing open, 18, 29
  textures and flavors of, 6–8, 10–11
  tracking, 21
  See also individual wines
wine clubs, 17
winemaking
  basics of, 12
  natural, 14–15
  Old World vs. New World, 13
wine shops, 16

Z

Zinfandel, 103, 139, 140, 142, 143

Published in the United States by Ten Speed Press, an imprint of Random House,
a division of Penguin Random House LLC, New York.
www.tenspeed.com

Ten Speed Press and the Ten Speed Press colophon are registered trademarks
of Penguin Random House LLC.

Library of Congress Cataloging-in-Publication Data
Names: Leahy, Kate, author. | Scott, Erin, photographer.
Title: Wine style : discover the wines you will love through 40 simple recipes /
    by Kate Leahy ; photographs by Erin Scott.
Description: First edition. | New York : Ten Speed Press, [2021] | Includes index.
Identifiers: LCCN 2020056299 (print) | LCCN 2020056300 (ebook) |
    ISBN 9781984857606 (hardcover) | ISBN 9781984857613 (ebook)
Subjects: LCSH: Cooking (Wine) | Wine and wine making. | LCGFT: Cookbooks.
Classification: LCC TX726 .L43 2021 (print) | LCC TX726 (ebook) |
    DDC 641.6/22—dc23
LC record available at https://lccn.loc.gov/2020056299
LC ebook record available at https://lccn.loc.gov/2020056300

Hardcover ISBN: 978-1-9848-5760-6
eBook ISBN: 978-1-9848-5761-3

Printed in China

Page 166: Author photo by John Lee

Acquiring editor: Lorena Jones | Editor: Emma Rudolph
Designer and art director: Emma Campion | Production designers: Mari Gill and Faith Hague
Prepress color and production manager: Jane Chinn
Food stylist: Lillian Kang | Food stylist assistant: Veronica Laramie
Models: Lilah Scott, Jillian Knox, and Otis Scott
Prop stylist: Erin Scott
Copyeditor: Kris Balloun | Proofreader: Rachel Markowitz | Indexer: Ken DellaPenta

10 9 8 7 6 5 4 3 2 1

First Edition